YORK NOTE

General Editors: Professor A........... (Uni....)
of Stirling) & Professor Suhei........ (*American*
University of Beirut)

Geoffrey Chaucer

THE PARDONER'S TALE

Notes by B.A. Windeatt

MA PH D (CAMBRIDGE)
Fellow of Emmanuel College, Cambridge

LONGMAN
YORK PRESS

YORK PRESS
Immeuble Esseily, Place Riad Solh, Beirut.

LONGMAN GROUP UK LIMITED
Longman House, Burnt Mill, Harlow,
Essex CM20 2JE, England
and Associated Companies throughout the World.

First published 1980
Third impression 1986

ISBN 0-582-78140-X

Produced by Longman Group (FE) Ltd
Printed in Hong Kong

Contents

Part 1: Introduction   *page* 5

   The life of Chaucer (c.1343–1400)   5

   Chaucer the poet   6

   The role of the Pardoners   8

   The medieval art of preaching   9

   A note on the text   11

Part 2: Summaries   12

   A general summary   12

   Detailed summaries   13

Part 3: Commentary   36

   The Teller and the Tale   36

   Chaucer and his sources   49

   Characterisation   50

   The Pardoner's last gamble   55

Part 4: Hints for study   58

   Some suggestions for detailed study   58

   Some key quotations   60

   Some questions and answers   64

Part 5: Suggestions for further reading   67

The author of these notes   69

Part 1

Introduction

The life of Chaucer (c. 1343–1400)

It is not known exactly when Geoffrey Chaucer was born. When he was a witness in a trial in 1386 he described himself as rather over 40 years old. His father, John Chaucer, was a wine-merchant in London, and Chaucer's grandfather had also been a wine-merchant. Chaucer's father and grandfather were successful men in their business, and were well thought of at court. We first hear of Chaucer in 1357 as a page in the household of one of the King's daughters-in-law, the Countess of Ulster. He was to be in various forms of public service for the rest of his life, a busy man of affairs as well as a poet. In 1359–60 he was taken prisoner by the French while fighting with the English army in France. He was released on payment of a ransom, of which the King paid part. In 1367 he started to receive a yearly pension from the King. Probably in the late 1360s he married Philippa Roet. She was a sister of Katherine Swynford, who later married John of Gaunt, the powerful fourth son of the King and a patron of Chaucer. So Chaucer was clearly attached to royal circles, and he continued to receive benefits and favours from the royal family. In 1368 he was again in France on military and diplomatic missions. In 1372–3 he visited Italy. From 1374–88 he lived in a house in Aldgate, London. In 1387 it seems that his wife died. In 1374 Chaucer was made Controller of the customs on wool in London. He was thus a civil servant, and an active one, because he had to keep the records of the customs in his own hand. Between 1376 and 1381 Chaucer was again involved on various diplomatic missions to Europe, including another visit to Italy in 1378. In 1377 on the death of his grandfather, Edward III, Richard II had become King, but Chaucer was kept on in his job at the customs. It is clear that Chaucer was regarded as a loyal and trustworthy servant to his king. In 1386 his job at the customs came to an end, possibly because of the influence of the King's enemies. But in the same year Chaucer was elected a Member of Parliament, although he only sat in Parliament for one year. In 1389 Chaucer was again given an important and hard job. He was made Clerk of the King's Works, and was responsible for all the King's residences. In 1391 he resigned from this position and was given responsibility for one of the royal forests in Somerset, in the West of England. In 1394 he was granted another royal pension, and in 1397 the King gave him a yearly gift of wine. When a new king, Henry IV, came to the throne in 1399, he continued the pensions and gifts to Chaucer. At the end of 1399, Chaucer leased a house in the garden of Westminster Abbey but died on 25 October 1400, and was buried in Westminster Abbey. Many later English poets have been buried near Chaucer's tomb in the Poets' Corner of the Abbey.

Chaucer the poet

It is clear from the record of his life that Chaucer was a poet in addition to leading a full professional life. It is of course likely that his success as a poet contributed to his success in the court circles in which he moved. He was well read in French literature and its influence appears in his poetry. His visits to Italy brought him into contact with the writings of the great medieval Italian poets, Dante, Petrarch, and Boccaccio so that he had a broad knowledge of contemporary European literature. But Chaucer has won his place in English literature—and he is often called, rather excessively, the 'Father of English Poetry'—because he wrote in English. From the conquest of England by the Normans in 1066 to the later fourteenth century, French was the language of courts and educated people. But by Chaucer's time the use of French was declining, even in the higher circles. It is Chaucer's achievement that he absorbs all the sophistication and the technical achievement of the French and Italian literature that he knew, and then builds on this to create his own poetry in English. The exact order in which he wrote all his works is now difficult to decide. But some of his earlier works such as *The Book of the Duchess* (1369) show the influence of French literature. This poem is a dream-vision, and Chaucer continued to write about dreams in his poems *The Parliament of Fowls* and *The House of Fame*. Several of Chaucer's works show marked Italian influence: his greatest single poem *Troilus and Criseyde*, written in the 1380s; and also *The Knight's Tale*. *The Knight's Tale* is the first of the great collection of stories, *The Canterbury Tales*. Some of these may have been written earlier, like *The Knight's Tale*. But others are perhaps Chaucer's most mature work and *The Pardoner's Tale* would be among them. *The Canterbury Tales* was left unfinished at Chaucer's death although it is still a large and unified work.

At the opening of *The Canterbury Tales* twenty-nine pilgrims find themselves in the same inn in London, all about to set out on a pilgrimage to the tomb of the popular saint, Thomas Becket, at Canterbury. They agree to travel together, and the innkeeper, the Host, offers to go with them and organise the telling of tales by the pilgrims to entertain each other on their journey. The teller of the best tale will receive the prize of a dinner on their return to London. The telling of all the tales, the return journey and the judgement, were never completed by Chaucer. But the character of the Host, and the nature of the pilgrimage and of some of the pilgrims, contribute to the effect of *The Pardoner's Tale*. The Host is a strong and vigorous character. Although he does not himself tell a tale, his character emerges strongly in the links between the tales. Here it is he who organises the pilgrims; it is he who chooses and controls who will tell a tale. He is a man of very strong reactions, but also earthy and very fond of jokes and amusement.

Among the pilgrims are quite a large number who have some kind of profession which involves them with the business of the medieval Church. Only one of these pilgrims, the poor Parson or priest, performs his profession as he should. Of the others, the Monk, the Friar, the Summoner and the Pardoner are all the special subject of criticism. It is against this background of comment in *The Canterbury Tales* on the officials of the Church and their shortcomings, that Chaucer's attitude to the Pardoner should be seen. There is a tradition that Chaucer was once fined for beating a Franciscan friar in London. And certainly, *The Canterbury Tales* expose how far the medieval Church fell short of its own ideals. But this does not mean that Chaucer was anti-clerical. Like other medieval critics of abuses in the Church, he is concerned with the abuse, not with the Church. The Church and its faith are man's hope. They are not questioned by criticism of Church officials. By attacking corruption Chaucer is commenting on how the Church's work is prevented by the same people who should be advancing it. But it is a sign of Chaucer's devotion to the Church that he presents such a favourable picture of the ideal priest. Chaucer's parson is a poor and humble man who follows his duty in caring for the spiritual health of the people for whom he is responsible. With the Parson, Chaucer is presenting his ideal of how the Church's work can be done. It is a path of simplicity and absolute honesty. And this is especially interesting for the contrast that it offers to the character of Chaucer's Pardoner. For in Chaucer's times it was often said that Pardoners were in business with the priests to make money out of poor people. Chaucer not only makes the actual Parson and Pardoner on the Canterbury pilgrimage into complete opposites, but he also repeats his Pardoner's boast of how he makes fools of the poor country priests that he visits. But perhaps it is time to say a little in explanation of the role of Pardoners in the medieval Church.

The role of the Pardoners*

To understand how the profession of Pardoner was created by the medieval Church, and how it became corrupted, it is necessary to recall the emphasis of the Church on the confession of sins, or wrongs committed against God by the individual Christian. The medieval Christian was to confess his sins regularly, and there were three parts to confession. First, one must be truly sorry (or contrite); second, one must confess one's sins fully to a priest; and third, one must perform the penance, or punishment, which the priest decides is appropriate to one's sin. Note that the individual priest does not have the power to forgive sins. In the view of the Church, only God can forgive. But the priest can signify that God has forgiven the sinner and so *absolve* him. Yet unless the sinner has sincerely performed all three conditions, then he is not forgiven.

There is a brave attempt here, in theory, to separate God's forgiveness from the work of God's agent, the priest. But it is not surprising that it was not always understood by simple people, who naturally jumped to the conclusion that it was the Church and its priests which could set their consciences at rest. And as time went on, the Church turned more to imposing financial penances instead of spiritual ones. Instead of doing good and holy works as a punishment, the individual could make some money or gift offering to the expenses of the Church. From this, it is a short step to the popular assumption that the forgiveness of God was something that could be bought and paid for. It can be unpleasant to spend money but it was less painful and troublesome than performing some more spiritual form of penance. Indeed, by the later Middle Ages, the Church had developed the notion that it was the guardian of a kind of bank or treasury in which the credit (in medieval terms, grace) which had been built up by the good works of all the dead saints, and through the lives of Christ and His Mother Mary, could be made available to sinners who needed grace. The theory, of course, demanded that the sinner should be truly sorry or penitent for his sins. But the more immediate practice demanded that he make a payment to the Church for the favour of this grace. It is scarcely surprising that true repentance tended to be forgotten in what had become a commercial transaction.

For so many good and necessary projects depended on the money

---

* On Chaucer's Pardoner and his times, see J.J. Jusserand, *English Wayfaring Life in the Middle Ages*, 2nd edn., London, 1889; A.L. Kellogg and L.A. Haselmayer, 'Chaucer's Satire of The Pardoner', *Publications of the Modern Language Association of America*, 66, 1951, pp.251–77; Jill Mann, *Chaucer and Medieval Estates Satire*, Cambridge University Press, Cambridge, 1973.

that was collected in this way, that business tended to take over. The care of the sick and poor in hospitals, new churches and roads were all financed by this trade. And to collect so much money, individual institutions needed to employ individuals to sell pardons on their behalf. These were the pardoners. They started as simple and lowly Church officials. They were forbidden to preach and they need not be priests, but could be laymen. But the pressures of commercial interest in what they were employed to do led to a long tradition of corruption. For in order to raise more money, they pretended to be more than they were. They became a scandal, and in fourteenth-century England pardoners are mentioned with scorn and hatred. In practical terms, it was impossible for the Church to control their activities in an age of poor communications, and their reputation became an embarrassment to the Catholic Church. The office of pardoner was abolished by the Church at the Council of Trent, in 1562.

When we look at Chaucer's Pardoner in the light of public opinion about pardoners, we can see how a figure who may at first sight seem exaggerated is entirely in keeping with the way Chaucer's audience would think of pardoners. He is completely free of any Church control, and he operates in remote country districts where the local people in their ignorance are easily deceived by him. In contradiction to the rules, he preaches in the pulpit like the priest. He uses forged documents to impress his audiences; and he sells them bogus relics and souvenirs of the saints. Most seriously, he has taken over the right to forgive people their sins. That is, he pretends to be able to take away people's guilt in return for payment. But really he was only able to take away some of their punishment. For only God could forgive their sins. But if simple people meet a grand, self-confident person with all the outward appearance of Church authority, and this man stands in church like a priest and says he is able to sell them forgiveness of sins in return for their offerings, then ignorant country people are not going to make the distinction. The general authority of the Church allowed the pardoners to exploit simple people's trust in it. And all the time, the Pardoner's own drunken behaviour is disgracing the institution that employs him, and his greedy readiness to take any form of valuables as well as money, in exchange for his pardons, involves him in a disgusting materialism, quite contrary to the originally other-worldly, spiritual emphasis of Christianity on the contempt of this present world and its goods.

The medieval art of preaching

Since the Pardoner gains his money by becoming a preacher, it will be necessary to understand something of the tradition of medieval preaching. To hear sermons was of course a very frequent occurrence in medieval life, and Chaucer himself must have listened to innumerable sermons during his life. He wrote one himself, which forms the tale told by the good Parson at the end of *The Canterbury Tales*. The Parson's sermon provides a suitably holy conclusion to the structure of the tales told on the way towards the great cathedral at Canterbury. The Parson's sermon is a good example of the complicated work of art which many medieval sermons became. Preaching the truths of the Christian religion was so important that it became surrounded with the rules of an art. Much of this art went into the organisation of the construction of the sermon. And this careful structuring can be seen in Chaucer's *Parson's Tale*. One reason for the care that went into a sermon's structure was because it would be listened to, rather than read. The listener needs different directions from those for a reader if he is to grasp the unity of what he is hearing. The reader can turn over a few pages and see before he starts the length of what he is beginning to read. The listener has no guide to the length or shape of what he is hearing. In sermons, a tradition of using a comparable structure in all well constructed sermons would help the listener to appreciate each part of the sermon and its relation to the whole.

The traditional medieval sermon tended to have six divisions, according to the advice given by manuals written in the Middle Ages to guide sermon-writers. The sermon usually started by stating its guiding text or theme, and then moved into an introductory section. It then returned to analyse its original text more closely before proceeding to give its illustration of the theme, in the form of an *exemplum*, an illustrative example or anecdote. The sermon then moved to discuss more particularly the application of its teaching, and concluded with a final blessing.

When we look at *The Pardoner's Tale* with this pattern in mind, we can notice how the structure of the prologue and tale follows the sermon pattern, although the Pardoner gives more emphasis to some sections than others. The Pardoner states his theme (lines 47–8)* and later returns to it (137–42). An exposition of some of the sins involved occupies the first part of the tale (199–374), after which follows the *exemplum* of the search for Death (375–632), the application of the anecdote (618–29) and something of a final benediction. Indeed, it

---

* line numbers refer to *The Pardoner's Prologue and Tale*, ed. A.C. Spearing, published by the Cambridge University Press in 1965.

would be surprising if the Pardoner did not use some of the structural patterns of sermons. He is, after all, presenting himself as an extremely effective preacher. But the role of these divisions in the prologue and tale should not be given too much significance for their own sake. Chaucer is more interested in creating the manner of a sermon, and in this the traditional transitions and divisions of the sermon are very effective in conveying the skill with which the Pardoner uses the art of preaching to manipulate his audience.

Chaucer has also carefully reproduced the method of argument of the skilful sermon. This is seen in the Pardoner's use of a style which builds up lists of examples to add to conviction, balancing statement with illustration. Above all, it is a style which compels assent. For the mastery of changes of speed and difficulty of language mean that more is emotionally accepted than is understood by a simple audience. Passages of tempting simplicity are mixed with much more questionable and obscure passages. But the feeling of a clear line and a consequent hold on the listener's attention and agreement is never lost by the Pardoner for his own purposes. It is an art of persuasion. And from the mouth of the proper person it could be an art to achieve the highest good of all for medieval man—the spiritual reformation and the continued inner growth of his soul. This is the ideal of the medieval sermon as an art of persuasion. But in the mouth of Chaucer's Pardoner on the pilgrimage of *The Canterbury Tales*—and in the mouths of the pardoners of Chaucer's England—it had become an art of extortion.

A note on the text

The text used throughout these notes, and the one to which all line-numbers refer, is *The Pardoner's Prologue and Tale*, edited by A.C. Spearing, Cambridge University Press, Cambridge, 1965.

Many manuscripts of Chaucer's poems circulated in medieval England, and *The Canterbury Tales*—including of course *The Pardoner's Tale*—were first printed by William Caxton in 1478, and again in 1484. A good edition of Chaucer's works was published by William Thynne in 1532, and another by Thomas Speght in 1598, which was revised in 1602 and much reprinted subsequently. Modern scholarship on Chaucer begins with the edition by Thomas Tyrwhitt (1775–8). W.W. Skeat's great edition (1894–7) is still respected, although F.N. Robinson's edition of *The Complete Works of Geoffrey Chaucer*, Oxford University Press, London; 2nd edn., 1957, has become the standard. A useful modern edition is *The Pardoner's Prologue and Tale*, edited by Nevill Coghill and Christopher Tolkien, Harrap, London, 1958, but note that the line-numbering differs slightly from that of the Spearing edition.

Part 2

Summaries
of THE PARDONER'S TALE

A general summary

In the introduction, the Host first expresses his reactions to *The Physician's Tale* and then calls on the Pardoner to tell his tale. The Pardoner agrees to do so when he has had a drink, whereupon the 'gentiles' (the upper-class pilgrims) protest they will listen to no filthy story. He undertakes to tell 'a moral tale'. But first in his prologue the Pardoner gives examples to the pilgrims of how he preaches to simple audiences and deceives them with false relics. He has no concern with their souls but only with his own profit. His text is always the same: 'love of money is the root of all evils'. With this he can make others repent of the sin of avarice that he practises himself. He will not work himself, while he can make a good living as a pardoner. But although himself 'a ful vicious man', he can tell the pilgrims a moral tale and will do so now he has drunk some ale.

The Pardoner begins to tell of some people in Flanders who lived riotously, drinking, gambling, and blaspheming in taverns. But he then interrupts his tale to preach against these young revellers' vices. First he deals with drunkenness using Lot and Herod as examples. Then he discusses gluttony. Then he returns to drunkenness, using Attila and Lemuel as examples. Then he preaches against gambling, illustrated by the experience of Stilboun (Chilon) and Demetrius. Finally, he preaches against swearing. Now he returns to his tale of three revellers in a tavern who hear passing by the funeral of a friend who has been killed by Death. They swear together to find Death and kill him. They rush off drunkenly and meet an old man who seeks in vain to die. He tells them where they can find Death and sends them down a crooked path. They find a hoard of gold coins, and forget all about looking for Death. They will guard the gold until they can remove it secretly at night, so they draw lots to find which of them is to go and fetch food and drink from town. The youngest is to go, and, after he leaves, the other two agree to stab the youngest when he comes back, and divide the gold between two instead of between three. But the youngest has decided to kill his two companions. He buys poison; borrows three bottles; poisons two, and keeps one for himself. When he returns, the other two stab him, but then drink the poisoned wine and also die.

The Pardoner cries out against their sins, showing how he uses the story to win money from his listeners. But then he tries to sell his pardons to the pilgrims themselves, and wants the Host to offer first. The Host refuses roughly and insults the Pardoner. The Knight steps in to reconcile them, and the pilgrimage continues.

Detailed summaries

The introduction to *The Pardoner's Tale* (lines 1–42)

The Pardoner's prologue and tale are introduced by the response of the Host to the preceding tale told by the Physician and his invitation to the Pardoner to tell the next tale. The tone of the tale is immediately determined by the vigorous swearing of the Host which opens the introduction to the tale. Although Chaucer presents the Host as a bluff, essentially masculine character, he also shows him subject to very strong emotional reactions. *The Physician's Tale*, which has just finished, tells the story of Virginia, taken from early Roman history. Virginia, a beautiful young girl, is one day noticed by a wicked and corrupt judge who desires to possess her. By the evidence of a corrupt subordinate, he is about to have her taken from her father, but Virginia's father kills her himself rather than surrender her to a life of dishonour. The people take the father's side and the judge is himself imprisoned. It is to this story, emotionally told by Chaucer's Physician, that the Host is reacting when *The Pardoner's Tale* opens. For some lines the Host can think of nothing else but the pathos of the girl's death and the wickedness of her enemies. He bursts out almost madly with oaths on the corruption of the judge and his partner and prays that all like them may meet a shameful end. It was Virginia's greatest gift, her beauty, that brought about her death. This moralistic idea obviously appeals to the Host for he repeats it twice. He also expresses repetitiously the more universal notion that the gifts men are given by nature and by chance bring about the death of many, or at least bring them more harm than good. And twice he repeats his comments on the pitiful nature of what he has just heard. This idea that we prove to be unfortunate precisely because we have gifts from Fortune will be an important theme of *The Pardoner's Tale*. Chaucer introduces it early on here in the mouth of the Host. But the Host is not a man to remain sad or emotional for long. He now turns to making fun of the Physician and the tools and terms of his trade, his medicines and prescriptions. In this part of the speech the Host uses many technical medical terms. The Host's manner is mocking, and his ironic apology suggests that we are to imagine that the Physician is taking offence during this speech, although Chaucer does not actually show him saying anything to the Host. With more oaths the Host goes on to claim that the tale has so moved him that he must have a drink of ale and must hear a cheerful tale to brighten him up after *The Physician's Tale*.

The Host now asks the Pardoner for a tale, addressing him in French as his *bel ami* (my good friend), with a courtesy that may well be ironic. The Host asks for something amusing. The Pardoner agrees readily, echoing the Host's own oath 'by St Ronyan'. But first, he insists on eating and drinking, for the pilgrims are just passing the signpost of an inn. At this the more well bred and refined pilgrims protest that they will not hear any filth from the Pardoner. Their literary taste is in keeping with their social status. He must tell them something morally edifying, some piece of wisdom to which they will gladly listen. He agrees but says he will have to think of an improving tale while he has a drink.

NOTES AND GLOSSARY

as he were wood: 'as if he were mad'. The Host's feelings are extreme.

Harrow! ... by nailes and by blood!: 'Alas ... by the nails of Christ's Cross and by Christ's blood'. The oaths play on the violence of Christ's crucifixion.

as herte may devise: 'As may be thought'.

Algate this sely maide is slain: 'Anyway this poor innocent girl is slain'.

yiftes of Fortune and of Nature: the distinction here is between natural endowments of Nature in soul and body, and the external, circumstantial gifts of Fortune (money and high rank).

of bothe yiftes ... Men han ful ofte moore for harm than prow: 'from both men very often derive more harm than profit'. The Host muses on the doubleness of these gifts.

passe over, is no fors: 'Let's not dwell on it, it doesn't matter'. The Host has recovered quickly from his emotions.

The Host's knowledge of medical terms: *urinals* (vessels for keeping urine); *jurdones* (chamber-pots); *ypocras*: this is both a common form of the name of Hippocrates (b. 460BC), the ancient medical authority, and also a wine flavoured with spices; *galiones*, a word only found here. The Host may be deliberately confusing a reference to Galen (*c.*AD130–*c.*AD200), the other famous ancient doctor.

boyste ful of thy letuarie: 'box full of your medicine'. The Physician apparently thinks the Host is being rude.

So moot I theen, thou art a propre man: 'As I hope to succeed, you are a fine-looking man'. The oath is so general as to be meaningless in Modern English, but it does suggest the Host's emphatic way of talking.

Seint Ronyan: possibly a corruption of St Ninian, an early British saint; although possibly a mock oath by the Host on the French word *rognon* ('kidney'), that is, 'By St Kidney'.

I kan nat speke in terme: the Host is slyly retreating from his earlier attempt to use the technical language of medicine.

myn herte to erme ... caught a cardynacle: 'You make my heart grieve so that I have almost had a heart attack'. *Cardynacle* seems the Host's own personal confusion of the medical term *cardiacle* with *cardinal*. He has some knowledge of medical words, but not enough to be always correct in his compliment to the Physician on the effect of his tale.

By Corpus bones! but I have triacle: 'By God's bones unless I have medicine ...' The Host, with his usual oaths, is finding an excuse for a drink.

The Pardoner's Prologue (43–176)

The Pardoner starts by describing his practice when he preaches in churches. He speaks out loudly, and as resoundingly as a bell. He knows by heart his biblical text or *theme* (47) which is always the same one: that love of money is the root of all evils (I Timothy 6.10).

The Pardoner then gives an account of the deceptions he practises on the simple people who hear him in church. He tells how he first shows his bulls, the official documents that provide him with authority to operate. At the start, in order to protect himself, he shows the people the seal of their local bishop ('oure lige lordes seel'), who has licensed the Pardoner. Then he goes on to show them spurious bulls from popes, cardinals, even the patriarchs. The Pardoner is persuading his audience to accept his credentials, before he plays on their simple faith for his own profit. So he works into his preaching a few Latin words to give it an air of holiness.

Now the Pardoner tells how his sales-talk begins, and repeats the words of his sermon. He displays glass boxes ('cristal stones') containing old rags ('cloutes') and bones which people think are relics of saints.

More particularly, the Pardoner is selling his country audience relics which will cure their animals of common illnesses. He has a sheep's shoulder-bone that supposedly belonged to a holy Jew. He claims that any animals harmed by worms, which drink from a well in which the bone is placed, will be cured. Sheep will also be cured of various skin diseases ('pokkes and scabbe') by drinking this water. But the well into which this 'relic' is put will have even greater power. If the man who owns the well will drink its water every week before the cock crows, then the number of his cattle will greatly increase.

With a remarkable transition, the Pardoner's sales-talk turns from saying the bone will multiply its owner's cattle to claiming that it will cure jealousy. This, of course, is directed to the wives in his audience. Even when a husband is crazed with jealousy, if his soup ('potage') is made with water from this well, he will never again suspect his wife. This will be so, despite the fact he knows for certain she has been unfaithful to him, even if she has been unfaithful with two or three priests.

The Pardoner now tries to sell a marvellous mitten, which, if used by a farmer when sowing his seed in the fields, will produce a much greater yield of grain.

The Pardoner's final trick is to suggest that those men who have committed sins so terrible they dare not confess them, and those women who have been unfaithful to their husbands, will not be able to make an offering for his pardon. But those who are innocent of such sins will be able to come to the front and spend their money on his relics. With this the Pardoner's example of his sermon concludes.

Turning again to the Canterbury pilgrims, he boasts how much money (100 marks a year) these frauds have won him every year that he has been a pardoner. He then goes on to describe how he preaches to the congregation and gives a picture of his own practice when standing in the pulpit. He compares himself to a dove in the way that he stretches his neck out to nod at the people, perhaps making every individual in the congregation feel that he is being personally addressed by the Pardoner. With a kind of professional pride, the Pardoner tells how both his tongue and his hands move busily (*yerne*). Clearly he is a persuasive preacher, using both gesture and eloquence.

His theme is always avarice, in order to persuade people to give away their money—to him. He admits he is interested only in his own gains and not at all in the battle against sin. Indeed, he cares less than nothing (he claims) about what happens to the souls of his audience after their deaths. The Pardoner claims defensively that much preaching is inspired by evil intentions in the preacher. Some preaching is inspired by flattery to please people, some by pride, and some by hatred. The Pardoner himself will speak ill of anybody who has criticised him or pardoners in general. He will not name the person he is attacking, but he will preach so that his audience will know very well whom he means. In this way he is able to revenge himself on enemies, while appearing very virtuous and holy.

Again, the Pardoner repeats that he only ever preaches out of covetousness, or desire for possessions, and thus he always uses the same biblical text ('The love of money is the root of all evils'). He preaches against the very same sin of which he himself is guilty. His skill as a preacher is such that he can persuade others to repent their avarice sincerely. But this result of his preaching is quite accidental to the Pardoner's own concern with winning the money of his audience.

Returning to the tricks of his trade as a preacher, the Pardoner tells the Canterbury pilgrims how he himself favours using old tales and examples in his preaching. This is because ignorant, uneducated people enjoy such simple stories which they can repeat and hold in their minds. The Pardoner asks the pilgrims why he should live and be content with poverty when by preaching he can gain gold and silver. He will do no menial or manual work to support himself. He is not going to imitate the simple life of Christ's apostles. He wants cash, wool, cheese and corn, even if it is given up to him by the poorest servant or the poorest widow in a village, and even if her children should starve for lack of food as a result. No indeed! The Pardoner chooses to drink his fill of wine and to have a willing girl in every town that he visits.

Finally, the Pardoner addresses the pilgrims at the end of his prologue. They want him to tell a tale. Now that he has drunk some ale he hopes he will be able to tell them something that will be to their liking, if he is able to please them at all. Even though he is himself a wicked and corrupted man, he is able to tell them a moral tale which is one he is accustomed to tell as one of his examples when he preaches for his own gain. If the audience will be quiet, he will begin.

NOTES AND GLOSSARY

whennes that I come: (He claims to come from Rome.) It was a common complaint that many pardoners claimed to be from there.

my bulles: 'my official documents with round seals attached to them'.

To saffron with my predicacioun: 'To give flavour and colour to my preaching'. The Pardoner's imagery is of the cook spicing and enhancing the taste of food.

in latoun: the sheep's bone is set in latten, hammered brass.

And nevere ... thre: The unfaithfulness of women and the immorality of priests are frequent matters for comment by medieval writers.

so that he offre pens or elles grotes: 'provided he offers pennies or groats' (a silver coin, worth fourpence).

By this gaude: 'By this trick'. Chaucer is not the first medieval writer to have referred to this trick of blackmail by pardoners.

An hundred mark: a mark was two-thirds of £1. The sum would be enormous by fourteenth-century standards.

As dooth a dowve sittinge on a berne: 'As does a dove sitting on a barn'. Some modern readers see an ironical reference here to the dove which is the traditional symbol of the Holy Ghost, the third part of the Trinity of God the Father, God the Son, and God the Holy Ghost. This depends for effect on whether one sees the Pardoner as a victim of despair, the most serious of all sins because a sin against the Holy Ghost.

Myn entente is nat but for to winne: 'My intention is only to make a profit'. The Pardoner boasts of his corrupt purpose.

'I do not care when they are buried whether their souls go to pick blackberries': to pick blackberries is essentially a wandering activity, finding the berries here and there. It represents the Pardoner's complete lack of interest in the fate of the souls of those he exploits.

Thus spitte I: The Pardoner compares himself to a snake when protecting himself and other pardoners from their critics. The imagery of snakes vividly expresses the strength of his hatred for any who dare to question his activities.

Ne make baskettes: there seems a confusion here between two saints called Paul—the relatively obscure St Paul the Hermit, who supported himself by making baskets, and St Paul, the great Apostle (or early missionary of Christianity). St Paul, the 'Apostle to the Gentiles' (that is, to the non-Jewish world) made a series of missionary journeys after his conversion to Christianity. He was eventually arrested and taken to Rome, where he died a martyr's death under the Emperor Nero (c. AD68).

That shal by reson been at youre liking: 'That will please you if you are reasonable people.'

The Pardoner's Tale: the scene is set (177-198)

First of all, the Pardoner sets the scene of his tale. Once upon a time in Flanders there was a group of young people who gave themselves up to debauchery and to gambling. They frequented brothels and taverns, where they danced to music and played at dice at all hours of day and night and where by their excessive eating and drinking in that devil's temple they worshipped the devil himself. All the time they swore great and wicked oaths on the different parts of Christ's body, as if they were themselves tearing Christ's body to pieces all over again, and as if they thought the Jews had not torn him enough. They were amused by each other's sins. All the dancing girls, market-girls, singers, prostitutes, and sweet-sellers who came into that place were really working for the devil, to draw the revellers into lechery, which is part of gluttony. The Pardoner now claims inaccurately that the Bible supports him in saying that sexual sin is linked with drunkenness.

NOTES AND GLOSSARY

In Flaundres whilom: 'Once in Flanders'. The Pardoner is setting his tale well in the past. Flanders (part of modern Belgium) was sometimes known for its drunkenness. The Flemish immigrants to England in Chaucer's time were not popular.

As riot, hasard, stywes, and tavernes: this line concisely presents the sins which concern the Pardoner. *Riot* suggests rowdy debauchery. *Hasard* is gambling in general, and also a particular game in which the gambler tries to guess the number before he throws the dice. *Stywes* (stews), means brothels; *tavernes* evokes the drinking that accompanies all the other sins.

Withinne that develes temple: Here the Pardoner suggests that, in their abandon and excess, the revellers turn the tavern into a church of the devil. They pay honour to the devil by their sin and lack of restraint. The tavern becomes an inversion of normal religious activity.

Oure blissed Lordes body they totere: notice the Pardoner's rhetorical approach to his audience. He and his audience are on the same side, reverencing Christ and hating those whose oaths by the various parts of Christ's body mean that He is re-crucified every time they swear.

The hooly writ ... dronkenesse: The Pardoner claims to quote the Bible in support of his statement that lechery (*luxurie*) and drunkenness are connected, because he wants to stress how any sin is part of all sin. But the Bible does not say exactly what the Pardoner says it does ('And do not get drunk with wine, in which is excess' Ephesians 5:18).

He preaches against drunkenness and gluttony (199–262)

Having established a scene of drunkenness and gluttony, gambling and swearing, the Pardoner now turns to giving warnings about each of these sins in general. As he himself predicted in the prologue, he uses well-known examples and stories to illustrate the dangers of these sins. He does not return to the story of the revellers in the tavern until later.

First, the Pardoner gives a series of examples illustrating the dangers of drunkenness. His first two cases are biblical. He reminds his audience of Lot, brother of Abraham, who was once so drunk that he slept with his two daughters. Secondly, he tells how King Herod, when he was drunk at a feast, gave an order that John the Baptist, the precursor of Christ, should be killed.

Now the Pardoner quotes approvingly the remark by Seneca (c.3BC–AD65), who said he saw no difference between a drunk man and a mad man, except that madness lasts longer than drunkenness. But, in an emotional outburst, the Pardoner reminds his audience that the original sin of Adam and Eve which first introduced corruption into the world was caused by gluttony. It was gluttony that drove Adam to eat the forbidden fruit of the Tree of Knowledge in the Garden of Paradise. And for that moment of greed, Adam and all his descendants were expelled from Paradise, to live in pain in this world until Christ bought back what men had lost by sacrificing himself for them. At what great price was Adam's greed bought!

And now the Pardoner comments, in a vivid passage, on the revolting nature of excessive eating and drinking, for if men knew what evils come from over-indulgence they would be more moderate in eating. What a great deal of labour and trouble is caused throughout the world by the need to grow enough food for those who eat too much! Here the Pardoner quotes St Paul against gluttony. In a vivid passage the Pardoner borrows from St Jerome, the great Father of the Church (c.AD340–420), to visualize the greedy man turning his own throat into a lavatory by his terrible gluttony. St Paul is again quoted on those who make their stomachs their god and who are the enemies of Christ.

With this, the Pardoner bursts into an address to the human stomach, stuffed with excrement and filth, emitting foul smells. He again draws attention to the inordinate trouble that is taken by armies of cooks to satisfy the human stomach. The Pardoner's description of cooking here draws attention to the mixture of softness, and of the variety of sauces through which the stomach craves luxury and novelty. But he who makes such pleasures the centre of his life is spiritually dead.

NOTES AND GLOSSARY

dronken Looth: the Pardoner recalls the biblical story of how Lot's daughters made their father drunk, in order that he would sleep with them unnaturally (*unkindely*) and gain grandchildren (Genesis 19:30–8).

Herodes, whoso wel the stories soghte: the Pardoner is confidently claiming his familiarity with the authoritative stories, and his manner does not invite contradiction. The Bible tells how Herod orders the execution of John the Baptist because of his vow to reward his step-daughter, who asks for John's head (Matthew 14, and Mark 6). But the Pardoner is using the Bible for his own ends, for Matthew and Mark do not actually say Herod was drunk, although he swears an oath he later regrets at a feast.

Senec seith a good word doutelees: In his 83rd letter, Seneca, the Roman stoic philosopher, calls drunkenness a voluntary insanity which differs only in duration from madness itself when madness has occurred in some wretched person (*yfallen in a shrewe*).

O glotonye, ful of cursednesse!: the Pardoner's first exclamation (or *apostrophe* in medieval rhetorical terms). Notice the effect in preaching. He balances the previous examples with an emotional generalisation on the sin of gluttony which includes all his audience in feelings of guilt.

lines 212–26:   The Pardoner now makes gluttony into the reason for man's expulsion from Paradise. Adam was disobedient when he accepted from Eve an apple from the Tree of Knowledge in Paradise. But the Pardoner is echoing St Jerome, who had seen Adam's sin as one of gluttony. The Pardoner associates the sin with the original cause of all human unhappiness, in order to manipulate his audience's strongest feelings against gluttony.

O wiste a man . . .: ('If one only knew . . .'). Now the Pardoner moves on, to represent the revolting waste of gluttony itself. Notice the emotive effectiveness of his quick transition from gluttony long ago in Paradise to the physical realities of too much eating and drinking. The Pardoner's language emphasises the delight of food and drink, but also how brief that delight is: 'the *shorte* throte, the *tendre* mouth'.

as Paulus seith . . .: The Pardoner is enlisting St Paul on his side: 'Food is meant for the stomach, and the stomach for food—and God will destroy both one and the other' (1 Corinthians 6:13). And a little later he is quoting St Paul again (243–7): 'For many, of whom I have often told you and now tell you even with tears, live as enemies of the Cross of Christ. Their end is destruction, their god is the belly, and they glory in their shame, with minds set on earthly things' (Philippians 3:18–19). Notice how the Pardoner is here quoting literally in his sermon, in order to take over for his own preaching the authority of the apostle Paul.

And turnen substaunce into accident: the Pardoner is using medieval philosophical jargon to describe the arts of cooking. *Substaunce* was the inward essence; the *accident* was the outward characteristics. The Pardoner suggests that cooking is an art of deception, masking the real nature of the food. But in the Catholic Mass, by the doctrine of transubstantiation, bread and wine become Christ's body and blood, although they still have the *accidents* of bread and wine. The cooking demanded by gluttons becomes a perversion of the transformation of the Mass.

But, certes . . . vices: The Pardoner here echoes St Paul again to bring the section on gluttonous eating to an authoritative close ('She who is self-indulgent is dead even while she lives', I Timothy 5.6).

He preaches especially against drunkenness (263–302)

Having dealt devastatingly with the evils of eating, the Pardoner now returns to the dangers of drink. He gives a vivid little portrait of a drunkard, whose breath smells nasty, and whose snoring is so heavy he seems to be crying 'Sampson! Sampson!', although of course the biblical hero Samson was bound by a vow to drink no wine (Judges 13–16). The drunkard falls as heavily as a slaughtered pig and loses his power of speech and his self-respect, because drunkenness is the tomb of a man's intelligence and discretion, and a drunkard can keep no secrets. The Pardoner urges his audience to beware of the mixtures of French and Spanish wines currently being sold in some of the main commercial streets of medieval London, such as Cheapside and Fish Street. They are so intoxicating that a man after two or three drinks will fancy himself in Spain rather than in London.

The Pardoner reminds his audience that, by contrast, all the major successes of the characters of the Old Testament in the Bible were achieved by prayer and the avoidance of drink. He recalls the warrior Attila, leader of the tribe of Huns who terrorised Rome in its last days, and who died in drunken debauchery (AD453). The Pardoner contrasts this with the instructions given in the Old Testament that those in positions of authority should not drink, in case it interferes with their duty to see that justice is done.

NOTES AND GLOSSARY

This wyn of Spaigne ... by: French wine was illegally mixed with cheaper Spanish wine. The Pardoner suggests ironically that this is because Spanish grapes come from a district situated near French wine areas, rather than for dishonest reasons. Here, the Pardoner is showing off his own shrewdness to the Canterbury pilgrims.

But herkneth ... leere: The Pardoner's preaching against drunkenness has been so far based on vivid particulars of the effects of drink. Here he alters his style of approach in a moment. He now claims sweepingly that all the victories in the Old Testament of the Bible were won because of prayer and abstinence from drink. Once more he invites his audience to check this up ('Looketh the Bible ... '), which is a way of showing his own confidence.

Attilla: so fluent is the Pardoner's technique that he does not illustrate the Old Testament victories through abstinence. Instead, he goes straight on to the example of a warrior like Attila who was destroyed by drink.

What was comaunded unto Lamuel: the Pardoner is again supporting his argument from the Bible, and refers to the Book of Proverbs: 'It is not for kings, O Lemuel, it is not for kings to drink wine, nor for princes strong drink; lest they drink and forget the law, and pervert the judgement of any of the afflicted' (31:4–5).

He preaches against gambling (303–342).

Having discoursed on gluttony, the Pardoner now moves to an attack on gambling, which he declares the cause of deceitfulness, lies, blasphemy and murder, as well as a waste of time and money. To gamble is also quite contrary to honour, and the more important the person the more damaging is the danger of gambling. Nobody thinks well of a ruler who gambles. To illustrate this, the Pardoner refers to an example from ancient Greece. An ambassador named 'Stilboun' is sent by Sparta to Corinth to make an alliance. But the ambassador finds the Corinthian rulers playing games of chance. He returns to Sparta and refuses to lose either his own honour or that of his country by allying Sparta with a country of gamblers. As another example, the Pardoner recalls how the King of Parthia scornfully sent to King Demetrius a pair of gold dice because he could not respect somebody who had been a gambler.

NOTES AND GLOSSARY

manslaughtre, and wast also/Of catel and of time: the Pardoner's list of the evils caused by gambling descends into anticlimax, from murder to waste of money and time. It is typical of the Pardoner's style of preaching that all sins are attacked as fiercely, regardless of their relative seriousness.

Stilboun: The story of the ambassador, Stilboun, Chaucer takes from *Policraticus* by John of Salisbury (*c.* 1115–1180), where he is called 'Chilon'. Chaucer seems to have thought the same philosophical ambassador also visited King Demetrius (335). Seneca's letters tell of how a philosopher called Stilboun met a certain ancient King named Demetrius.

He preaches against blasphemy (343–74)

From this, the Pardoner proceeds to the last part of his sermon on the sins, which is an attack on swearing of oaths. Here the Pardoner's sermon is heavy with quotations from the Bible. First, he quotes from St Matthew and then from Jeremiah, and concludes with the relevant commandment of the Ten Commandments, against swearing. From the early position of this commandment in the order of the Ten Commandments, it is suggested that to misuse the name of God is an even greater sin than murder itself. The Pardoner echoes another biblical quotation in declaring that he who swears scandalously will never escape from punishment. The Pardoner then gives some examples of some of the offensive swearing by the body of Christ. These oaths are made even more wicked by the trivial or the criminal contexts in which they are used: to express impatience or indignation in gambling quarrels, or to accompany threats of violence and murder. Concluding that so many grave sins come from gambling with dice, the Pardoner ends the first phase of his tale by begging his audience to avoid oaths.

NOTES AND GLOSSARY

Witnesse on Mathew: the last part of the Pardoner's sermon, on blasphemy, is supported by a string of biblical references; first to St Matthew: 'Again, ye have heard that it hath been said by them of old time, Thou shalt not forswear thyself, but shalt perform unto the Lord thine oaths. But I say unto you, Swear not at all ... ' (Matthew 5:33–4). So the Pardoner starts with Christ's teaching, reported by Matthew, against any form of swearing.

The hooly Jeremye: the Pardoner now builds on this by quoting Jeremiah closely from the Old Testament: 'And thou shalt swear, the Lord liveth, in truth, in judgement, and in righteousness' (Jeremiah 4:2).

'Take nat my name ...': Now the Pardoner supports his argument against swearing with one of the Ten Commandments, given to Moses on two tablets of stone on Mount Sinai. The commandment (*heeste*) against swearing is the second, according to Roman Catholic numbering, and so is on the first of the two 'tables' (353).

as by ordre, thus it stondeth: because the commandment against swearing comes before that against murder, the order of the Ten Commandments suggests blasphemy is more serious than murder.

That vengeance ...: The Pardoner again echoes a biblical text: 'If he swear in vain he shall not be innocent, but his house shall be full of calamities' (Ecclesiasticus 23:11).

Examples of oaths being used in gambling: 'The blood of Crist that is in Hales': refers to Hales Abbey in Gloucestershire, which claimed to have some of Christ's blood. It was a place of pilgrimage. Here it is being used as an oath by dice players. French numbers were used (*cynk and treye*).

The tale; the discovery of the gold (375–489)

Having now set the sins of the tavern in a moral perspective, the Pardoner returns to his story of the revellers in the tavern. The Pardoner had first set the material scene of the tavern and its debauchery, then he had set the moral scene by his sermon on the sins associated with taverns. His audience is prepared to see the exemplary quality of the story he is now starting. The scene is immediately one of debauchery. The three revellers are already sitting drinking before the earliest church bells ring at six in the morning. But they hear a different bell, being rung in front of a funeral procession. One of the revellers tells his servant to find out the dead man's name. But the boy has already heard that it is an old companion of his master's. He was slain as he sat drunk by that secret thief who is called Death, who is killing thousands of people in that region during the plague. The boy warns his master to be prepared for that enemy before he meets him. The boy's mother had advised him so. The innkeeper supports the boy's story. Death has killed many in a nearby village. It must be Death's dwelling place. It would be wise to be prepared.

With several oaths the reveller makes light of the danger and proposes to seek out Death. He proposes to his companions that they swear themselves brothers to kill Death. They pledge themselves to his brotherhood. Then they jump up in a drunken fury, and set off for the village mentioned by the innkeeper. They swear violent oaths, which tear Christ's body all over again. Death shall die if they can catch him!

They have not gone half a mile when they meet an old and poor man, just as they are about to climb over a stile. The old man greets them humbly and piously. The haughtiest of the revellers returns the greeting roughly and rudely and asks the old man why he is so wrapped up in his clothes, so that only his face can be seen. He also asks him why he has lived so long? After gazing into the young man's face, the old man answers that he lives because however far he travels he cannot find any man who will exchange his youth for the old man's age. And so he has to keep his old age as long as God wishes. Death does not choose to take his life, and so he must walk on like a wretch who cannot find peace. Always, he goes tapping with his stick on that ground which is the gateway to our mother earth. He begs to his mother to let him in. His body is shrinking and disappearing with age, and he begs for his old bones to rest. He would give all his clothes just for a shroud to be wrapped in. But his mother has not yet heard him, and so his face is pale and withered.

He then rebukes the young men for their rudeness. He quotes the Bible on the need to respect the old, and advises them not to injure any old man now, just as they themselves would not wish to be harmed when they are old. He is about to say goodbye to them politely, blessing their journey and pursuing his own inevitable course.

But the reveller rudely will not allow him to go before he tells them where they can find that Death which they have just heard him talk about. The young man accuses the old man of being Death's spy. He threateningly demands to be told where Death is, and accuses the old man of being one of Death's party, who wishes to kill young people.

The old man tells him that if they are so keen to find Death they should take the crooked path to a nearby grove. The old man has just left Death there under a tree, and Death will not run away. Indeed, Death will not hide himself because of the young men's confidence. In a final blessing the old man prays that Christ, who redeemed mankind by sacrificing himself, will save the young men and make them better.

So the old man finished and all three revellers ran until they reached the tree where they discovered what they thought to be nearly eight bushels of gold florin coins. No longer then did they seek after Death but sat down by the glittering coins.

NOTES AND GLOSSARY
The Pardoner's revellers hear a funeral bell instead of the early-morning church bell.

Looke that thou reporte his name weel: the namelessness of the revellers contrasts with their interest in the dead man's name. But they do not hear it. They hear only the name of Death itself, which has taken the dead man.

It was me toold er ye cam heer two houres: this is mysterious, and suggests Death's sinister control. Death was at work long before the revellers thought of it.

With his spere: in the middle ages, death was frequently visualised as a skeleton with a spear, and sometimes as a decayed, talking corpse. In the form of plague, death was such a frequent visitor that it is less surprising that the child and the inn-keeper speak about it almost as if it were a known character.

Goddes armes ... Goddes digne bones ... Goddes dignitee: note how the revellers' vow to kill Death is proposed with a string of blasphemous oaths. The three are from the start being characterised by their language.

Al dronken in this rage: the Pardoner emphasises that they act under the influence of drink which partly accounts for their confusion.

And Cristes blessed body al torente: the Pardoner repeats for emphasis his earlier idea (189), that blasphemous oaths tear Christ's body over again, and here specifically condemns the revellers for this sin. The contrast lies between Christ's real victory over Death on the cross, and the revellers' confused attempt to kill Death themselves. If the revellers could only understand what Christ has already done, they would see their own needless stupidity, and would stop hurting Christ by their oaths.

What, carl, with sory grace!: *Carl* is a contemptuous and derogatory word for *man*; *with sory grace* means 'bad luck on you' or perhaps 'curses on you!'. In short the reveller is abrupt and rude to the old man.

though that I walked into Inde: 'even if I walked as far as India'. India to medieval Europeans was the furthest extent of the world in popular talk.

Ne Deeth, allas, no wol nat han my lyf: the passive attitude of the Old Man towards death contrasts stongly with the active and aggressive search of the young men. The Old Man longs for death, but he is not literal-minded.

with yow wolde I ... : The idea of exchanging all his clothes willingly for a shroud is handled in a way that conveys the Old Man's great age.

But, sires, to yow ... : The Old Man uses the Bible to support his request for the proper respect of youth for old age. He is quoting a text in the Old Testament which runs: 'Thou shalt rise up before the hoary head, and honour the face of the old man, and fear thy God' (Leviticus 19:32).

if that ye so longe abide: a sinister hint: the Old Man urges the young to behave to him as they would themselves like to be treated when old, if they survive long enough for the question to arise! But death is common and they may never reach old age.

thider as I have to go: previously the Old Man's travels have seemed wandering, but here he suggests mysteriously that he is travelling towards an end.

By God ... by Seint John ... By God and by the hooly sacrement!: the young man's rough accusations are once more sprinkled with blasphemy. In the face of all this rudeness, the Old Man is no more than polite. He answers the young man's request for directions, the directions to Death.

this croked wey ... in that grove ... Under a tree: the setting is symbolic, yet clearly visualised. The crooked path is representative of the way of sin. The Old Man has chosen to leave the money in the grove. There is grim irony on how money will neither hide from nor fear the revellers.

No lenger thanne ... : The way in which the revellers 'forget' their quest for Death, because in fact they have found it in money, is the central image of the tale. It is the more powerfully conveyed by being expressed indirectly ('they did not seek any longer for Death'). The understatement expresses the delusion of the revellers.

The conclusion of the search for Death (490–608)

The very 'worst' of the revellers is the first to speak. He claims that he is clever even if he does like a joke. This discovery of money is a gift from Fortune to enable them to spend the rest of their lives in happiness. Since it came so easily, it will easily be spent. He exclaims, with an oath, on their unexpected good luck. Since they have found it, the gold is theirs, and they will be in luck when it has been transported to the home of one of them. But they must move the treasure by night, otherwise they will be accused of being thieves and executed for their own possessions. Two must stay with the money to guard it. A third will go to town to bring them bread and wine to last them until nightfall. They will draw lots as to who should go. As chance has it, the lot determines the youngest will go to town, and he leaves.

As soon as he has gone, one of the revellers remarks to the other friend that he only has his friend's profit at heart. Their gold is to be divided three ways, but, if it only needed to be divided between the two of them, would not that be a friendly thing? The second reveller does not at first understand. The first swears him to secrecy. He then proposes that when the youngest returns, the second reveller should pretend to start a friendly wrestling match with him, and while this is happening both of the older revellers will stab the youngest to death. Then the gold will only need to be divided two ways: they will have as much as they want and be able to gamble freely. They agree on this plan.

Meanwhile the youngest of the revellers is walking to the town thinking of the bright coins, and thinking how happy he would be if he could have all the treasure to himself. And so the Devil is able to put into his mind the thought that he should buy poison to kill his two friends. The youngest reveller sets his mind on this and has no intention of repenting his decision. Indeed, he hurries to a chemist and asks him to sell him some poison to get rid of his rats, also to kill a polecat in his back yard that has killed some of his chickens. He very much wanted to revenge himself on vermin that was doing him harm at night.

The chemist promises him something that will kill any creature in the world, even if it only eats or drinks of the poison an amount as small as a grain of wheat. Yes, any creature that eats it will die, and in less time than it takes to walk a mile at a normal pace, so strong and fierce is the poison.

The damnable reveller takes the poison in a box and hurries to a man in the next street from whom he borrows three bottles, putting poison and wine into two and keeping the third bottle of wine for himself. He was planning to work hard all that night transporting the gold from its hiding place. And so he returned to his companions.

As the Pardoner says, what happened afterwards does not need to be told at length. The youngest reveller was murdered exactly as the others had planned, and afterwards the two older revellers sat down to drink wine and amuse themselves before getting rid of the body. And as it happened one reveller picked up a poisoned bottle and drank, and gave some to his companion. And so both died. But the Pardoner supposes that neither Avicenna nor any other great doctor ever described any more terrible symptoms of poisoning than were endured by these two villains before they died. And so the two murderers and the poisoner all died.

NOTES AND GLOSSARY

This tresor hath Fortune unto us yiven: the Host's remarks on the fatal beauty of the heroine of *The Physician's Tale* (in the Introduction of *The Pardoner's Tale*) have already commented on how double-edged the gifts of Fortune and Nature can be. Besides, the revellers commit a crime in deciding to keep the found gold. Legally, they should report it to the authorities.

Hoom to myn hous, or elles unto youres: The 'worste' of the three is already aware of the need to divide the gold.

for oure owene tresor doon us honge: sudden, unexplained increase in wealth would be suspicious, and was sometimes taken in the middle ages as a sign of an undisclosed discovery of treasure.

breed and wyn: these are common enough foods, but they are also, of course, the Body and Blood of Christ in the Mass, and it is possible that the Pardoner is blasphemously linking the youngest of the three with Christ who was sent to earth to save man.

Shal it be conseil?: ('Shal it be a secret?'). Notice how the 'worste' reveller leads the other into temptation, by seeming to share his thoughts with him confidentially.

I shal rive him thurgh the sides tweye: the details of the proposed murder enable us to visualise it vividly, although when it happens the Pardoner says little of it (595). The Pardoner is more interested in the temptation and motivation to sin, than with its carrying out. But the detail of the knife through the third man's side could be intended to recall how Christ was wounded in the side on the cross.

For-why the feend . . . : The devil finds the youngest of the three is in such a wicked way of life that he is able, with God's permission, to lead him towards damnation. The youngest is fixed and resolute in his own wicked intention. He is completely without that hope of improvement, that could come with the readiness to repent of one's wickedness.

His rattes: the youngest man's lies to the chemist show his wickedness: he thinks of his friends as vermin, to be killed like animals who interfere with the profits of keeping chickens.

The pothecarie answerde . . . : the chemist's speech of professional pride in the efficiency of his poisons emphasises the dangers of such skills when they are available for sale. The chemist has no way of knowing the youngest man's real intentions, and this makes his pride in his poisons even more horrifying.

This cursed man . . . : The details of the youngest man's cunning plans are set against our own knowledge that all his cleverness is going to come to nothing. This is specially brought out by the note (587–9) that he made sure one bottle was full of unpoisoned drink, because he would need it himself when working hard at carrying away the gold. The youngest man's vain preparations suggest the blindness of human attempts at anticipation of events.

What nedeth it to sermone of it moore?: ('What need is there to speak any further of it?'). The contrast between the Pardoner's fullness of detail about the youngest man's plans, and his abrupt dismissal of the horrible deaths of the three is strikingly effective. The plans of their own wickedness are self-fulfilling.

Avycen Wroot nevere in no canon, ne in no fen: a device of detachment. The Pardoner is suggesting the deaths of the three were even more horrifying than those described in one of the great medical text-books of the Middle Ages, the work of Avicenna (Ibn Sina, 980–1037). Avicenna's *Book of the Canon in Medicine* is divided into sections named *fens* and uses the word *canon* to mean a rule of procedure. The Pardoner is once more making a show of his learning. Its effect is to stress the final agonies of the three wretches, but in a clinical and distant way, which prepares for the ensuing general exclamations.

How the Pardoner exploits his story (609–29)

Here the Pardoner has an outburst exclaiming against the sins that have figured in his tale, exclaiming against treachery, murder, gluttony, lechery, gambling and blasphemy. How, he asks, can man be so unfaithful and unnatural to his creator, the God who made him and bought him again from damnation by the sacrifice of his own blood?

With this the Pardoner has reached the emotional climax of his tale. The use of the story of the revellers has clinched his opening sermon against the sins that his audience have watched being practised by the revellers and at last destroying them with a terrible justice. It is at this point, accordingly, when his audience are most impressionable, that the Pardoner moves into what is for him the point of his preaching—the financial exploitation of his audience's emotions of repentance. He now launches into a prayer that his audience be preserved from avarice and cleverly holds out to them the chance of safety, a safety they can buy by purchasing one of his pardons. He urges the audience to come forward and exchange their belongings for one of his pardons, which has the power to save them from sin. It does not matter whether they offer money or whether they offer instead silver valuables (or even any of that wool which was such an important product of medieval England). The climax of the Pardoner's promises comes when he guarantees entry to Heaven to those who offer and are entered in his records. Quite wrongly, he assumes the power to absolve his customers from all their sins since childhood.

NOTES AND GLOSSARY

Here the Pardoner exclaims on all the sins involved in his tale. He starts off in a general vein. But note how he brings his general emotion round to end in an emotional appeal which plays on the feelings of each individual in his audience.

or elles silver broches, spoones, ringes: it is recorded in complaints about them that pardoners were prepared to take valuables instead of cash from the faithful. It was by such means that the sale of pardons came to resemble a market-place.

Youre names I entre: the Pardoner's whole approach to his ignorant audience exploits his superiority in literacy. To be entered on the pardoner's roll is a passport to Paradise.

I yow assoille . . . born: The last words of the Pardoner's 'model' sermon contain his most serious effort to mislead the ignorant. He claims outright the power to absolve them from all sin. This completely ignores the distinction between God's forgiveness and the priest's control over penance.

The Pardoner turns to the pilgrims . . . (629–82)

At this point the Pardoner appears to turn back to the Canterbury pilgrims, explaining that this is the way that he is accustomed to preach. They have seen an example of his preaching and he prays that Jesus Christ (who is the doctor of our souls) will allow them to receive His own pardon. The Pardoner declares he does not want to deceive them; that that is best.

But now the Pardoner returns to his sales-talk once again: only this time he is using it directly on his colleagues on the Canterbury pilgrimage who have just listened to his account of his dishonest practices. He has forgotten to mention before that he has some relics and pardons in his bag which the Pope has given him personally with his own hands! The pilgrims can either come forward now devoutly and kneel to receive his pardon, or else they can acquire new pardons at every mile as they journey onwards. They can do either, as long as they keep on offering good money. Because of the accidents that may occur, it is an honourable thing for the pilgrims to have an excellent pardoner to absolve them as they journey through the country. After all, one or two of the pilgrims may fall off their horses and break their necks! Let them only consider what a safeguard it is to them all that he happens to have become one of their company, when he is able to absolve them from their sins, whatever their social status, if any of them should die.

Having directed his sales-talk at the Canterbury pilgrims, some impulse now drives the Pardoner to choose the Host, as the member of the pilgrimage whom he wants to win over as his first customer. He starts by trying to enlist the rest of the pilgrims on his side against the Host by irony. He declares it is his advice that the Host should be the first to offer money for a pardon, because he of all the pilgrims is most sinful. Let the Host open his purse and offer some money!

But the Pardoner has misjudged his man, and is the object of a speech from the Host which, for its concentrated vigour of obscene abuse, has no rival in Chaucer. The Host declares he will be damned if he will pay. The Pardoner would try to make the Host kiss the Pardoner's old breeches and swear they were the relics of a saint, even though they were stained with the Pardoner's excrement. The Host swears with an oath that he would rather have the Pardoner's testicles in his hands than relics. Let them be cut off! Just as a relic of a saint is put into a shrine, the Pardoner's testicles will be put into a shrine of pig's excrement.

The Pardoner is so enraged at this deluge of insult that he will not speak another word, and the Host declares he will no longer deal with any short-tempered man. But the gracious knight, when he notices how all the pilgrims are laughing, steps in to smooth the quarrel. He urges the Pardoner to cheer up and most politely asks the Host to show he reconciles himself to the Pardoner by kissing him. Similarly he asks the Pardoner not to stand aside, and urges that the former good humour be restored. So Host and Pardoner kissed, and continued on their way.

NOTES AND GLOSSARY

Whiche were me yeven by the popes hond: The Pardoner's claim that his pardons and relics were given him by the Pope himself is of course absurd, but it shows the ambitiousness of his selling-technique. He is now gambling himself, and gambling for complete victory.

It is an honour . . . : after showing the pilgrims, by his own account, what a criminal he is towards ignorant peasants, the Pardoner now tries to persuade his middle-class audience that it is an honour for them to have his services available to them. The change of tone is breath-taking, and so is the consistency and confidence with which the Pardoner tries to persuade the pilgrims. He even tries (649–52) the approach of the insurance-salesman, for his pardons are a spiritual insurance in event of broken necks on the pilgrimage journey to Canterbury.

But, by the crois which that Seint Eleyne fond: St Helena, mother of Constantine, was thought to have discovered the true cross on which Christ had been crucified. Relics of wood from the True Cross were objects of veneration in the Middle Ages. The Host refers to the True Cross with a characteristic oath, in the middle of his attack on the Pardoner's false relics. For the Host is far from attacking all relics, only the frauds. His instinctive swearing by the True Cross, in order to express the strength of his rejection of the Pardoner's relics, emphasises the Host's attachment to true relics.

But right anon . . . : Although the Knight is the pilgrim of highest social standing, the competition of tales is under the Host's organisation. But now that the Host has himself become emotionally involved, the Knight steps in to settle the argument by the authority he possesses through his rank. His great courtesy to the Host is noticeable. Not only does he say the Host is dear to him (678), but he also addresses him in the polite plural form, ('I prey yow that ye kisse the Pardoner'). This is his good manners to the organiser of the pilgrimage. The contrast with his address to the Pardoner ('And Pardoner, I prey thee, drawe thee neer'), where he switches to the singular form, sums up in a line the inferiority and isolation of the Pardoner on the pilgrimage.

Part 3

Commentary

The Teller and the Tale

It will always seem difficult to write about *The Pardoner's Tale* of Chaucer. The story is so compelling and Chaucer presents it with such terrible force, that many a reader will feel that its main pleasure communicates itself in the act of reading, and that modern writing about the tale can only clear up points of detail. It is true that the story of the three young men's search for Death has this terrifying simplicity in itself. The form and structure of the story *are* its meaning and leave little more to say. But the story of the search for Death is only part of the total structure of *The Pardoner's Tale*. Although it does form what the Pardoner would himself call his tale, it forms only a part of the whole. While the story is the climax which completes the unity of the tale in meaning and form, we also have to consider the larger framework of preaching by the Pardoner within which the tale of the search for Death is presented.

The Pardoner's Tale is so powerful in itself that it can be enjoyed on its own, but it has a much greater meaning when we realise we are reading what is part of a much larger collection of Chaucer's poems, *The Canterbury Tales*. It was a device of medieval poets and story-tellers to have a group of people telling each other stories. The great Italian poet and author Giovanni Boccaccio (1313–75) uses this frame-work for his collection of tales *The Decameron* (1353). A group of young ladies and gentlemen, who are staying in the country because there is plague in Florence, tell each other stories. Similarly, Chaucer's *Canterbury Tales* are told by a group of pilgrims on the journey from London to the tomb of St Thomas Becket at Canterbury Cathedral. (Becket (*c.*1118–70), as Archbishop of Canterbury, defended the rights of the Church against King Henry II, his former friend. He was murdered by supporters of the King and made a saint in 1172). Chaucer's pilgrims make an agreement to tell stories to each other to pass the time, and in competition for the prize of a dinner when they return. But it is Chaucer's originality that he gives vivid, memorable characters to most of the tellers of his stories. Chaucer gives life and character to the setting in which his tales are being told, as well as to the tales themselves. Of all these characters, the Pardoner is one of the most vivid and most unpleasant, and it is in showing off to the other pilgrims his corrupted skills as a preacher that the Pardoner spends much of his tale.

Chaucer is presenting *The Pardoner's Tale* within two frames. It is part of the larger unity of *The Canterbury Tales*, but within that large frame the tale itself must be seen as framed by the character of the Pardoner who is telling it. The tale does not exist for itself, as it did in the folk-tale versions in which Chaucer probably knew it. It exists as part of a performance by the Pardoner in which he demonstrates his preaching skills. The whole structure of Introduction, Prologue and Tale is designed so that the tale reflects back on its teller.

This is in character with all of Chaucer's major poetry. He was clearly a superb story-teller, but his interests went wider. The device of dramatising the character of the teller of a story enables Chaucer not only to tell the story but to offer a perspective on it. He uses stories not only for the value of the stories themselves, but for the way in which the telling of the story becomes part of its meaning. The tale of a search for Death, in which Death is found as money, is striking in itself. Its fascination becomes compelling when we watch this story being rehearsed by a pardoner, who uses it to persuade others to save themselves by giving their money to him, while he himself remains unmoved by the lesson of his own tale in his greed for money.

The Pardoner in the *General Prologue*

Because, in the greatest *Canterbury Tales*, the form of Chaucer's tales is so closely linked with their tellers, we should use all the evidence Chaucer gives us on the character of the Pardoner.* For his character can illustrate why he tells the tale as he does. Chaucer's main description of the Pardoner comes in the *General Prologue* to *The Canterbury Tales*, where Chaucer describes each of the pilgrims in turn. It is significant that the Pardoner is the last of the pilgrims to be described, along with the other more unsavoury pilgrims, the Miller, the Manciple, the Reeve, and the Summoner (who is a fr'end of the Pardoner's). But the Pardoner comes last of all, and there is the suggestion that his corrupted profession, combined with his unpleasant character, makes him an outcast on the Canterbury pilgrimage.

Chaucer's description in the *General Prologue* builds up by suggestive details an impression of a social and personal outcast. First, Chaucer

* G.G. Sedgwick, 'The Progress of Chaucer's Pardoner 1880–1940', *Modern Language Quarterly*, I, 1940, 431–58.

tells us the Pardoner is connected with the hospital of St Mary Rouncivalle, near Charing Cross in London, a cell of the convent of Roncesvalles in Spain. Pardoners who collected money for hospitals governed from abroad were especially difficult to control. There had been several recent scandals connected with the Pardoner's Rouncivalle, and Chaucer probably wants to associate his Pardoner with this bad publicity. The Pardoner is pictured riding along singing a love song ('Come hither, love, to me!') in company with the odious Summoner. Summoners were minor ecclesiastical-discipline officers, whose own corruption allowed the corruption of pardoners to flourish. Chaucer works most subtly by placing significant observations near to each other, and leaving his readers to make the connection. Here, there is a strong suggestion, but no statement, of an unsavoury relationship between the two men. Certainly, Chaucer immediately places us on our guard about the Pardoner by saying he has come directly from Rome. It was one of the complaints about contemporary pardoners that they claimed authority direct from Rome in order to impress simple people. In his Tale we see the Pardoner making more use of this.

The Pardoner as Eunuch

Chaucer's description of the Pardoner's personal appearance is calculated to suggest effeminacy. Medieval man thought that specific features of personal appearance had a scientific relation to the individual's character. The study of physical appearance had consequently developed a tradition of interpretation, and it has been found that the details Chaucer describes in his Pardoner would be taken by the medieval observer as the outward signs of a eunuch.* The Pardoner's lank and revolting hair is the first of these details Chaucer notices:

> By ounces henge his lokkes that he hadde,
> And therwith he his shuldres overspradde;
> But thinne it lay by colpons oon and oon   (677–9)

So the Pardoner's hair hangs in what Modern English would call 'rat's tails'. The other details Chaucer notices are more obviously revealing. The Pardoner has the glaring eyes of a hare, an animal some medieval scientists thought could be hermaphrodite. Moreover, the Pardoner has a thin voice like a goat's, and he has no beard at all 'nor never would have'. After these hints, Chaucer suddenly states his meaning more bluntly. He describes the Pardoner's sexual deficiency in terms of the

* W.C. Curry, *Chaucer and the Mediaeval Sciences*, Barnes and Noble, New York, 1960, ch.3.

language of the stable ('I believe he was a gelding or a mare'—691).

But there is the further possibility that Chaucer's account of the Pardoner's physical shortcomings as a man suggests a corresponding spiritual deficiency in him.* Chaucer, or his audience, would scarcely be unaware of the use of the eunuch as a symbol which Christ Himself had made in His teachings. Christ had declared that there were three types of eunuch: the eunuchs from birth; men made eunuchs by other men; and those who have spiritually made themselves eunuchs for the sake of the Kingdom of Heaven (Matthew 19.12). Some medieval commentators on the Bible developed further the spiritual symbolism of the eunuch, so that men who were *opposite* to those who made themselves eunuchs for the Kingdom of Heaven's sake were also eunuchs. They were eunuchs in the sense that although they had the opportunity to receive the truths of the Church, they chose not to put them into effect, indeed to waste them. It is possible that Chaucer sees in his Pardoner both a *physical* and a *spiritual* eunuch. This is in keeping with his perversion of what could have been a spiritually beneficial profession. He could be seen as refusing, in the traditional Christian language, to leave behind the 'old man' of sin and become the 'new man' in Christ. In this case, the Pardoner's love of the new, of the latest fashions, would be another grimly ironic observation. For when, in the *General Prologue*, Chaucer describes the Pardoner riding gaily along in the latest fashion ('al of the newe jet'), the irrelevant material novelty of his outward appearance contrasts with the dark, unreformed quality of his inward spiritual blindness.

The Pardoner's Relics

The other major concern of Chaucer in his description of the Pardoner's character is the Pardoner's use of bogus relics as part of the tricks of his trade. The empty character of the eunuch, and the cheap trickery with which his outwardly holy work is carried on, are the two principal and complementary features of Chaucer's picture. The Pardoner plays on the simple faith of country priests and their congregations. The medieval reverence for relics and the desire to possess them were so strong that the Pardoner finds easy markets for the old pillow-case which he says is the veil of the Blessed Virgin Mary, or the piece of sail he claims is from the boat from which St Peter tried to walk on the sea towards Christ (Matthew 14: 22–33), or the glass case full of pigs' bones which he presumably claims as the bones of saints. No wonder

---

* R.P. Miller, 'Chaucer's Pardoner: The scriptural eunuch and The Pardoner's Tale', *Speculum*, 30, 1955, 180–99.

Chaucer describes what a splendidly confident figure the Pardoner always cuts in church. For the appearance of self-confidence is essential to the confidence-trickster. And Chaucer's Pardoner is an ecclesiastical confidence-trickster. Indeed, it is possible that Chaucer makes him more brazen in his use of false relics than even contemporary pardoners could be. This is literary licence perhaps, to emphasise the nature of the frauds and forgeries of relics that did exist. As a monster, Chaucer's Pardoner is larger than life.

The context of the Pardoner's prologue and tale

Behind this façade of self-confidence, the motivations of the Pardoner in his professional life, and as these affect his tale, are more complex and uncertain. We have noticed how necessary for the effectiveness of *The Pardoner's Tale* is its setting in the Canterbury pilgrimage as a whole. For the relationship between the Pardoner and the other pilgrims is an important factor both at the beginning and the ending of his tale. In this way, the context of the pilgrimage governs the way the tale exists and works. The character of the Pardoner and the way the other pilgrims react to him decides the nature and course of the tale. And yet the precise location of *The Pardoner's Tale* in the order of *The Canterbury Tales* has been the subject of some argument. The tales of the Physician and the Pardoner are linked together dramatically as a sequence within *The Canterbury Tales*. It is the Host, as organiser of the competition of tales, who arranges the sequence. But there is no indication of where this fragment of two linked tales should be placed in the pilgrimage. In the early manuscripts it is found in a number of different positions in *The Canterbury Tales*. This is curiously apt for the Pardoner, whose nature and calling mean that he does not really belong anywhere. He is unspeakable, and he is also peripheral to the society of pilgrims. He has been compared to those grotesque figures which medieval artists included in the margins of religious manuscripts, and medieval sculptors included in the surface decoration of the great cathedrals.* The medieval mind acknowledged the existence of the ugly and the incongruous and found a place for it, even tucked into the midst of holiness. Chaucer has also found a place for a grotesque figure, but leaves uncertain his relationship to the pilgrimage as a whole.

The other pilgrims, particularly the more refined, have already formed some judgement on the Pardoner's character by the time he begins his tale. They consider him prone to drink, as well as to his other vices. The

---

* D.R. Howard, *The Idea of The Canterbury Tales*, University of California Press, Berkeley, California, 1976.

combination of drink and his corrupted character makes the better-class pilgrims fear they will have to listen to a filthy story, for they protest when the Pardoner insists on stopping at a tavern before telling his tale. The Pardoner has already been rash enough to interrupt the Wife of Bath in her Prologue, and her withering reply assumes he has been drinking. The protest of the better-class pilgrims at the start of his tale is interesting, because of what impression it suggests that they have formed of the Pardoner up to this point. They have already heard a number of low-life stories, including one by the drunken Miller. It may be that they just happen to decide to draw a line when it is the Pardoner's turn. Yet their reaction against him can be seen as more urgent and particular than that. It suggests that some other pilgrims have a particular loathing and distrust of this particular pilgrim. To a character whose life and work depend on confidence and conviction, this is a peculiarly intense situation. Perhaps this is why Chaucer shows us the Pardoner saying:

'I graunte, ywis,' quod he, 'but I moot thinke
Upon some honest thing while that I drinke'   (41–2)

Since he goes on to use material that he claims to know by heart, there is no reason why he should pause to think here. He is certainly not thinking of 'som honest thing'. Chaucer is possibly suggesting how the Pardoner decided to respond to the suspicion of the *gentil* pilgrims. His own professional success depends on an ignorant country audience. On the face of it, there is no way in which he could hope to persuade in the same way the much more sophisticated and mixed society of the pilgrims. Nor can he hope that they will see him as the noble Church figure that simple country people do. In the present company he has nothing left to display but the sheer technical achievement of his eloquence. Persuasion of the reality of what he says so eloquently—and with it, social status—would seem denied him by the *gentils'* response. But in his character, the Pardoner must display. He is always driven to win that influence which admiration can give.

The Pardoner's prologue and tale is consequently a self-conscious performance of literary art by the teller of the tale. It no longer matters to the Pardoner whether he reveals to the pilgrims the secrets of his frauds. Indeed, he recklessly gives himself away, precisely in order to draw their attention to his technical virtuosity. The effect of the Pardoner's performance on us has been compared to the effect of watching an actor in a play, whom we have just previously heard boasting backstage of his powers to move an audience to laugh or cry. Indeed, in *The Pardoner's Tale* we see something more chilling and more unnatural. For we watch an actor performing, whose only existence lies in his skill in falsification. It is Chaucer's greatest irony that the very material which the Pardoner excels in using is material which condemns the Pardoner himself. This economy of irony can be achieved because it is the tradition of preaching that the Pardoner is perverting. So it is only the glittering shell of a preaching technique that the Pardoner provides in response to the *gentils'* request for an 'honest thing'.

The Pardoner's prologue

Once we accept that the tale is founded in a desire to exhibit preaching technique, then much of the structure and style of the tale falls into a much more coherent pattern. The prologue becomes the Pardoner's statement of his underlying text. More especially, the first phase of the tale, in which the Pardoner preaches against various sins of drunkenness, gluttony, gambling and blaspheming, becomes an integral part of the tale. It is by no means a digression from the narrative, once we recognise that one of the unifying factors in the tale is the Pardoner's self-exposure as a preacher.

The subject of *The Pardoner's Tale* is thus in large measure himself, and the Prologue encourages this impression by centring itself in the Pardoner's own experience. His first words plunge us into his life of deceptions, stressing what an effective performer he is:

'Lordinges,' quod he, 'in chirches whan I preche
I peyne me to han an hauteyn speche ...'   (43–44)

And he loses no time in stating that he knows his preaching by heart and so, presumably, knows by heart what he is saying now to the pilgrims. His perennial theme ('Love of money is the root of all evils') is stated at the outset and then followed by the Pardoner's list of the tricks. By these, his own greed for possessions is satisfied from other people's desire to escape sin, but also from their own greed. For the appeal of many of the Pardoner's fraudulent relics is that they will enrich those who are holy enough to buy them. A sheep's shoulder bone which is such an effective medicine for animals would be very desirable to a farming man, and so would a mitten that magically increased the yield of corn. The Pardoner is clever enough to realise that his ignorant audiences want to save money, as well as appear pious. His contempt for their stupidity is obvious in the ludicrous nature of his claims, for only fools could be taken in by them. This is brought out by his sales-talk on the cure for jealousy: the medicine will stop a husband distrusting his wife even if he knows she is untrustworthy. It is impossible not to despise your customers who will believe this. And if the people's stupidity will not help his profits then blackmail can, as is shown by the Pardoner's trick of suggesting that only hardened sinners and adulterous women will be prevented from taking advantage of his relics.

Chaucer gives such zest to the Pardoner's account of his tricks that here, as throughout the tale, the fast pace suggests the Pardoner is being carried away by his own speech. Having established his superiority over his simple victims, he moves on to set against this his own essential detachment from the supposedly holy work he is performing. Chaucer is characterising the Pardoner's professional pride. He is now rushing on to give the picture of himself that he wants to see: the effective professional operator. He boasts of his vast earnings. He gloats over them and glories in them not only for their magnitude but because they have been so easily won:

> By this gaude have I wonne, yeer by yeer,
> An hundred mark sith I was pardoner   (103–4)

And his confidence and sense of mastery of his profession lie behind his words:

> I stonde lyk a clerk in my pulpet   (105)

For this is a small but characteristic example of the Pardoner's belief in the power of nerve and eloquence for gain. He is not a cleric and he is usurping the parish priest's pulpit for his own purposes. He is, of course, able to make the people think of him as a cleric in his own pulpit. The sheer exhilaration in his own fraudulent profession has the power to fascinate even modern readers, who have no preconceptions of the pardoner's role. It is the commitment to energetic performance that draws our imaginations—the rapid, darting movement of the head, like a dove's, the speed of the tongue and the hands. Because we have been shown all this outward energy, the Pardoner's inner detachment becomes more shocking by contrast, when he remarks with complete indifference:

> I rekke nevere, whan that they been beried
> Though that hir soules goon a-blakeberied!   (119–20)

All the energy of the previous lines is cut short with this callous remark. The Pardoner's energetic preaching technique is instantly shown to be only skin deep.

It is the irony of the tale that, because a perversion of preaching is involved, the Pardoner may be able to do good, although this is quite contrary to his interest in preaching for his own gain, and is also quite incidental to him. This paradox of an art which can achieve its purpose contrary to the intention of the artist is a necessary part of the ironies of the tale, to which it will be necessary to return later. The only place where the Pardoner's language does suggest that he is totally involved in his preaching is when he tells how he preaches against those whom he hates for attacking himself and other pardoners. The vivid imagery of snakes is employed here:

Thanne wol I stinge him with my tonge smerte ...   (127);

Thus spitte I out my venym under hewe
Of hoolinesse, to semen hooly and trewe   (135–6)

The language is so strong that it suggests the Pardoner is now really roused. It contrasts strongly with his indifference to the ignorant folk. What rouses him to hate is the confidence-trickster's fear of those who have gone against him. For any opposition is dangerous to that complete conviction which is necessary for him to operate.

What is fascinating in the Pardoner's prologue on his professional practices, is the consciousness of what he is doing. It is his frankness about himself that holds the reader's attention. It is the Pardoner himself, after all, who openly declares:

Thus kan I preche again that same vice
Which that I use, and that is avarice.   (141–2)

The mode of confession by a character is a feature of other medieval literature. Chaucer's Wife of Bath would be one example. In her long prologue she gives an extended description and defence of her own experience of married life. A possible model for Chaucer in *The Pardoner's Tale* was the character of 'False-Seeming' in the great medieval French allegorical poem *The Romance of the Rose*, part of which Chaucer himself translated into English. The character called False-Seeming certainly gives a lengthy account of his deceptions and hypocrisies. Because he is a character within the scheme of an allegorical poem, he tends to be endowed with more hypocrisies than any individual character's life and role could produce or sustain, and this is no disadvantage within the French poem's allegorical intentions. Chaucer's use of confession for several of his characters is more interesting in human terms.* This is because he limits their experience to some specific area. He also makes their frankness a kind of perverse pride, which goes hand in hand with a certain very human obtuseness. In this way, we have the curious pleasure of meeting a character who is

---

* P.M. Kean, *Chaucer and the Making of English Poetry*, Routledge and Kegan Paul, London, 1972.

devastatingly clever, but to whose cleverness we can also see limitations. The Pardoner is clever enough to be able himself to see the ironies in his position:

> But though myself be gilty in that sinne,
> Yet kan I maken oother folk to twynne
> From avarice   (143–5)

He is even able to argue why he should bother to imitate the holy lives of Christ's apostles, when he can acquire money so effectively. His confession of motives engages us with its frankness. And there is no need to think it unrealistic. We can all think of how readily strangers will speak of themselves to others, often with an embarrassing frankness. With Chaucer's Pardoner, the frankness gains its force from the triumphant presentation of his own cruelty in pursuing his profession. He will control and exploit the weak; he will have money

> ... of the povereste widwe in a village,
> Al sholde hir children sterve for famine   (164–5)

The Pardoner is certainly proudly frank about his own wickedness. Yet all his show of self-knowledge can only be expressed in a way that ironically comments on his ignorance. His self-knowledge is sterile.

The Pardoner's Tale

The reader cannot reach *The Pardoner's Tale* itself without seeing it as intimately connected with the character and purposes of its teller. The opening scene of debauchery in the tavern links back to the theme of the Pardoner's own drinking. Indeed, he mentions having just had a drink of ale at the end of his prologue. Some readers have seen the Pardoner actually telling his tale—with its preaching against drunkenness—inside the tavern where he has had his drink. There is no explicit reference in the poem to support this, and the last line of the tale ('Anon they.kiste, and riden forth hir weye') could be taken to mean the pilgrims have been on horseback throughout the tale. Chaucer does tend to forget the setting of the tale-telling in *The Canterbury Tales*, except where this is particularly significant. If a tavern setting were to be imagined for the Pardoner's performance, Chaucer would probably have mentioned it. In any case, the preaching against drunkenness is only part of the tale, not the whole. The Pardoner's stop at an inn before he tells his tale is probably enough to suggest his own involvement with the world of taverns. Even in his drunkenness, there is the hint of extravagant performance and boasting:

Nay, I wol drinke licour of the vine,
And have a joly wenche in every toun.   (166–7)

His drinking is associated with his sexual boasting, and this at least we know must be an empty boast.

Preaching as preface to the tale

Within *The Pardoner's Tale* itself, approximately the first third is taken up by the Pardoner's examples of his preaching against those sins of the tavern scene with which he opened. It is only after his preaching that he returns to his narrative of the search for Death. This is the example of that short and memorable tale which he has already said is most effective in preaching to ignorant audiences. The story of the three revellers is consequently being used for the Pardoner's purpose, in order to give tangible narrative form to the dangers of the sins that he attacks, particularly avarice.

Thus, when the modern reader eventually reaches the story of the three revellers, his way of reading should have been shaped by the moralising viewpoint of the earlier part of the tale. The characters of the revellers and the other minor characters then take on a symbolic, emblematic significance. For it is the method of the preaching introduction to the tale to see the universe in terms of moral examples. The lives of characters in the past are recalled because of the moral lesson that can be extracted from their fate. The arguments against the sins are the performance of a skilful exercise, which shows the Pardoner completely in control of his material, but also in control of its emotional effects on the listener. Notice how the Pardoner interrupts the strict course of his argument to lay hold on his listeners' feelings. He does this with a liberal use of exclamations. He exclaims against the sins, their various effects, and also against the sinners. The alternation of teaching and exclamation is an insidious feature of the Pardoner's methods of persuasion. For the exclamatory passages help to enlist the listener's emotions in agreement with the preacher and so make his teachings seem more inevitably right.

Who would not agree with the Pardoner as he exclaims against these sins? For there is no disagreeing with the terms in which he condemns them. And he well knows the effectiveness of repetition. In his methods, the Pardoner is making use of traditional features of medieval preaching.

It was an art in which the accumulation of example was a stylistic strength. For the audience of a medieval sermon favoured a weight of 'authorities' behind the precepts conveyed by the sermon. As we would expect, the Pardoner employs the traditional manner, although more slickly than most contemporary preachers. He accumulates a body of examples for each type of sin. He introduces quotations from St Paul to support his teaching:

> Of this matiere, o Paul, wel kanstow trete:
> 'Mete unto wombe, and wombe eek unto mete,
> Shal God destroyen bothe', as Paulus seith.   (235–7)

He parades a knowledge of the Bible infinitely impressive to an ignorant audience:

> And over al this, aviseth yow right wel
> What was comaunded unto Lamuel—
> Not Samuel, but Lamuel, seye I;
> Redeth the Bible, and finde it expresly ...   (297–300)

Who would argue with a man so in command of his Bible that he can warn his hearers against misunderstandings? The Pardoner's confidence in his methods is well-founded. It is an impressive performance which proves the correct moral conclusions. It becomes even more impressive, in a different way, as the Canterbury pilgrims watch a thoroughly evil man proving the right moral conclusions, which still have no effect on him.

The opening of the tale

The form of the Pardoner's preaching, then, is authentic, and this guides the reader's response to his *exemplum* of the attempt to kill Death. But the sins attacked by the Pardoner can all be seen to be grimly relevant to the story of the three revellers. The structural pattern of the three sins underlies the story itself. The last sin of the Pardoner's sermon—blasphemy—provides the first turning-point of the story. Those who blaspheme by swearing casually on the parts of Christ's body are wickedly associating the name and character of God with their own degraded and trivial circumstances. Only somebody indifferent to the power of language could blaspheme, because he would be unable to appreciate the terror of what he was saying. The word became divorced from its reality. Preachers tried to counter this by warning that those who blasphemed on aspects of Christ's body during His Crucifixion were guilty of inflicting the same punishments on God all over again. This persuades people of the link between the words and their reality. In *The Pardoner's Tale*, the three revellers are also unable to link the word 'Death' with any reality they already know. This is wonderfully done by Chaucer, when he makes his three revellers misunderstand the child. The child thinks of Death as the traditional personification of much medieval art, who takes his victim by surprise and strikes him with his spear:

Ther cam a privee theef men clepeth Deeth,
That in this contree al the peple sleeth,
And with his spere he smoot his herte atwo,
And wente his wey withouten wordes mo.   (389–92)

And when the inn-keeper supports the story of the child, he similarly uses figurative language which contributes to the confusion of the revellers. He tells them that Death has destroyed the inhabitants of a nearby village and adds:

I trowe his habitacioun be there.   (403)

This habit of personifying an abstract idea like Death is beyond the drunken revellers' understanding and they assume a personification must be a person:

Deeth shal be deed, if that they may him hente!   (424)

The revellers are the victims of a terrible literalism. The evils of drink must be partly to blame in clouding their understanding. But their incessant blasphemous oaths also show they are blind to anything but the literal and material appearance of things.

It is Chaucer's achievement that he creates such a balance between the specific and realistic, and the general, that the events of the story seem both vividly particular and infinitely symbolic. The scene in the tavern illustrates this balance. It is striking that the three revellers are never given names, even though this is sometimes awkward. Their namelessness seems part of Chaucer's plan: it gives the story a more general tone. Similarly, the revellers ask the child to find out the corpse's name, and although he already knows before they ask him, he does not tell them the name. This is part of the mysterious quality of the scene. Yet, on the other hand, there is something very real and vivid about the noise of the funeral bell clanging through the street. By contrast, the child's speech is so universally applicable, so solemnly general, that it seems more than any particular child would say about death:

And, maister, er ye come in his presence,
Me thinketh that it were necessarie
For to be war of swich an adversarie.
Beth redy for to meete him everemoore;
Thus taughte me my dame; I sey namoore.   (394–8)

So assured does this seem that some readers have seen the child as symbolic and think he is referring to the Church, often thought of as our Holy Mother Church, when he speaks of advice from 'my dame'. Chaucer has prepared the way in the tale so efficiently that its characters can seem to have this symbolic, emblematic identity. On the other hand, there is nothing more natural and human than the way the innkeeper interrupts to support what the child has said:

'By seinte Marie', seyde this taverner,
'The child seith sooth . . .'   (399–400)

It is by this alternation of the concrete and the mysterious that the tale's style gives the work as a whole a both vivid and haunting impression.

Chaucer and his sources

That the story should open in a tavern is one of Chaucer's main changes to the traditional forms of the story he uses for *The Pardoner's Tale*. The overhearing of the funeral outside and the decision to kill Death are also Chaucer's way of visualising a start to the tale. All this contrasts with the older versions of the story, where the gold is discovered accidentally and without forethought. In his story Chaucer wants to emphasise how the three revellers consciously decide to set out to find and kill Death. In the older stories, the gold certainly turns out to be the death of those who find it. For they decide to kill each other, as in Chaucer. But it is Chaucer who extends the paradox by seeing his revellers as actually looking for Death.

In one version of the story, which Chaucer may have known, the story starts when a hermit finds some gold in a cave.* He runs away from it, but meets three robbers. They ask him what he is running from (because they see nobody following him). He tells them he is running from Death, which is chasing him. He agrees to the robbers' request to show them Death. When the robbers find the gold they call the hermit a fool. It is agreed that one robber shall go to town to fetch food and drink. But the devil puts into the mind of this robber that he could poison his companions and keep all the treasure. In his absence, the other two decide to kill him, and do so when he returns. They eat the food he has brought and die. This is how God rewards traitors. The robbers found death; but the wise man ran away.

* From a novella in the *Libro di novelle e di bel parlar gentile* (1572), but the story is thought to go back to earlier sources. See *Sources and Analogues of Chaucer's Canterbury Tales*, ed. W.F. Bryan and G. Dempster, Modern Language Association of America, Chicago, 1941.

Another version of the story shows how easily it could be used for moralising purposes.* Here it becomes part of the teachings of Christ. Christ is walking in wild country with His disciples. They see some gold coins and want to take them. But Christ refuses to let them take what would rob them of their souls. He promises that they will understand this when they come that way again. Now the story follows. Two friends find the gold. One goes to bring a mule to carry it; the other guards the gold. The first returns with a mule and two loaves for his friend. The friend refuses to eat, kills his friend when he is not looking, then gives the mule one loaf and eats the other. Both die. When Christ returns, He shows His disciples the bodies as predicted.

The example of these popular versions of the same story can help us to understand what Chaucer wants to emphasise in his own tale. There are some significant differences in structure and character. Chaucer's opening scene and the decision to kill Death produces much greater irony in the Tale. Chaucer's revellers do not recognise the gold as Death, even though they are looking for Death and have been directed specifically to that spot in order to find Death. Chaucer's version becomes more horribly intense. The blindness of his revellers becomes absolute, and their damnation more complete. Their madness is unforgettably represented as a kind of instant forgetfulness:

Ne lenger thanne after Deeth they soughte   (486)

Chaucer's version of the story reflects the Pardoner's own cynicism about the consuming greed that governs human nature.

Characterisation

The Old Man

The comparison with the other stories helps us to notice the next distinctive feature of Chaucer's tale. This is the character of the Old Man whom the revellers meet. It is clear that Chaucer wants the reader to notice this figure. He has more to say in Chaucer's tale than in the other stories, yet his relationship to the gold is more mysterious. There has been much argument about his meaning, and many explanations have been offered. Some see him as an allegorical figure of Old Age, the harbinger of Death. Some see him as the 'old man' (*vetus homo*) of Christian teaching, the unreformed aspect of mankind. Some see him as the Wandering Jew; that is, the traditional representation of the

* From a novella in *Lo ciento novelle antike* (1525), another Renaissance collection of older stories. See Bryan and Dempster, *Sources and Analogues*.

Jew always condemned to wander the earth without a home. Some claim that he is only a single old man, without any particular symbolic overtones.*

The fact that so many explanations are possible suggests that Chaucer did not intend any one of them to apply exclusively. The Old Man remains mysterious, and he is more effective in the tale because of this. Here again, we can notice how Chaucer has combined touches of concrete vividness with the hint of infinite significance. The effect reminds us of the child in the inn, and this contrast between innocent youth and dispirited old age is part of the completeness of the tale's vision. The tapping of the old man's stick on the ground—like the ringing of the funeral bell—brings him vividly present before our eyes. But it is never possible for us after reading this tale to see an old man with a stick, without thinking of the imagery of knocking for admittance to death. And this endows a simple action with a universal, emblematic significance about human life. This combination of the particular and the universal is more generally true of the characterisation of the Old Man. Every detail convinces us of his presence, but also has the power to suggest the figure of the Old Man is more significant than any individual old man. The way that he is wrapped up in his clothes – 'Why artow al forwrapped save thy face?' (432) – can suggest both an old man who feels the cold and also a corpse already prepared for burial. The long look which the Old Man gives the reveller: – 'This olde man gan looke in his visage' (434) – is a realistic gesture. But it also suggests more generally the greater wisdom and reflectiveness of old age as compared with youth.

Indeed, the characterisation of the Old Man develops as a series of contrasts with the young revellers. He is old and they are young. He speaks meekly, while they speak proudly. He speaks respectfully to the young; they speak very roughly and rudely to the old man. Both old and young are seeking Death; but the old man seeks Death as a release from life. The old man is poor and would give up what he has, while the young want more. The old man accepts God's will, whereas the young are indifferent to it. The old man uses religious language in order to call down God's blessing; but the young use religious terms only to swear and blaspheme.

Chaucer very effectively uses direct speech to distinguish between the attitudes of the old man and the young revellers. Chaucer concentrates on a confrontation between the Old Man and just one of the revellers. It is important that this is described as 'the proudeste of thise

* For an account of the possibilities, see J.M. Steadman, 'Old Age and Contemptus Mundi in The Pardoner's Tale', *Medium Aevum*, 33, 1964, pp.121–30.

riotoures three' (430), for the contrast with the humble old man could not be stronger. The Old Man greets the young politely, but the proud reveller replies in a very off-hand way:

' . . . What, carl, with sory grace!'   (431)

and goes on to ask the Old Man why he has bothered to live so long. Chaucer's direct speech shows all the spiteful ignorance of everyday rudeness. Yet the contrast it expresses between the resigned courtesy of old age and the shortsighted confidence of youth is greater than a particular time, setting, or character.

The long reply of the Old Man on why he remains alive offers a vital contrast to the outlook of the young. He longs for death, but he does not actively seek it, which would be a sin in Christian terms. He has discovered that nobody will give anybody else their youth in exchange for age, but that the individual must accept the conditions of his own life. It is this acceptance of things as they are that contrasts with the absurd activeness of the young. The Old Man is resigned, although this does not mean life is any less terrible. But his resignation is based on *awareness* and it is this which distinguishes him from the revellers.

By contrast with the Old Man, the young man's speech is monotonously rough and ugly, of course reflecting the ugliness of his soul. This contrast is very strong where the Old Man quotes the Bible on the need to reverence the old and is greeted by a mouthful of oaths:

'Nay, olde cherl, by God, thou shalt not so . . .
Thou partest nat so lightly, by Seint John!'   (464–6)

With a crescendo of blasphemy, the proud young man presses the Old Man to reveal where Death is:

'Telle where he is, or thou shalt it abye,
By God, and by the hooly sacrement!'   (470–1)

And the reveller accuses the Old Man of being Death's spy.

The character of the Old Man now takes a new turn. Previously he has been himself waiting for Death to take him. But he is now able to send others to find Death. There is no inconsistency here, at the level on which Chaucer's tale is working. For in his resigned old age, the Old Man knows better than to be tempted by that form of spiritual death which is represented by a concern for money. But he makes no attempt to stop those who cannot see the distinction between spiritual and physical death from finding both through the gold. The Old Man contains both the mercy and the justice associated with God, although the young do not see the distinction in what he is and says. If they had understood the first part of his speech, they could have changed their attitudes. But they continue the same, as is shown by the proud and blasphemous speech. Since they have ignored the possibility of change and mercy, then there is no alternative but justice. It is to this that the Old Man sends them. The character of the Old Man is certainly ominous, for he is a figure almost from the grave, between life and death. He provides mystery and reverence at the moment which is the turning point of the tale.

The three 'Riotoures'

The last phase of the tale itself deals with the effect of the new-found money on the three revellers. It shows Chaucer developing their characterization as a means of illustrating the development of sin. It has been said that there is only one character in *The Pardoner's Tale*, and that character is Death itself. There is certainly a negative quality about all the characters in the tale, in the sense that they all live in the shadow of death. Death is a powerful off-stage character, shaping the lives of the characters we see. In the three revellers, Chaucer is interested in those parts of their character which lead to sin and death. It is noticeable how Chaucer characterises the three young men through direct speech, because he is interested in showing how their motives develop. Events, by contrast, are less interesting.

So as soon as the three find the gold and sit down by it, Chaucer has 'the worste' of them suggest a plan in a long speech. He is proposing a criminal act, for under English law the discovery of the gold should be reported. Thus, Chaucer is showing in this speech how money leads to deception and fraud. The way in which this speech follows immediately on finding the gold has a speed which, although it is not unrealistic, contributes to the symbolic atmosphere of all action and event in *The Pardoner's Tale*. The division between money and crime and fraud is almost unnoticeable.

The conversation between the two who remain to guard the treasure is another most effective way of using direct speech to reveal the process of corruption of character by sin. Chaucer snows how the more wicked character leads on the less intelligent by flattery and pretended kindness. It all sounds so simple, logical, and harmless:

> But nathelees, if I kan shape it so
> That it departed were among us two,
> Hadde I nat doon a freendes torn to thee?   (527–9)

The second man does not understand immediately his friend's murderous plan, and Chaucer beautifully catches his misunderstanding in his speech:

> That oother answerde, 'I noot how that may be.
> He woot wel that the gold is with us tweye;
> What shal we doon? What shal we to him seye?'   (530–2)

The effectiveness of this speech is of course that we, unlike the second young man, immediately understand that the 'worst' young man does not intend to *say* anything to the youngest when he returns, but simply to murder him. We see our minds jumping to the same possibility as quickly as the 'worst' young man. And we are horrified and fascinated to see how terribly quickly money becomes the death of those who have any part in it.

It is especially noticeable how deception and pretence is tied up even with murder. There is nothing to stop the two young men jumping on the third and killing him. But they plan a way in which they will kill him by trickery in what seems a friendly game:

> Aris as though thou woldest with him pleye,
> And I shal rive him thurgh the sides tweye
> Whil that thou strogelest with him as in game,
> And with thy daggere looke thou do the same.   (541–4)

There is a pointless deceitfulness here for its own sake. The insistence that *both* should join in the murder makes it a terribly deliberate and conscious crime. And this same elaborate deceit marks the youngest man's preparations to kill the other two. Firstly, Chaucer makes his motivation by the devil rather more complicated than the other versions, which suggest simply that the devil put the idea into his head. Chaucer goes on to say:

> For-why the feend foond him in swich livinge
> That he hadde leve him to sorwe bringe.
> For this was outrely his fulle entente,
> To sleen hem bothe, and nevere to repente.   (561–4)

So Chaucer's young man is so wicked that this is why the devil is able to put the murderous plan into his head. There is not a trace of regret. It is a conscious, deliberate intention. This fixed purpose makes especially horrible the details of his shopping and his preparations for the poisoning. The invented story about the rats to be killed, the shopkeeper's boastful pride in the superior killing power of his poison, the careful preparation of the bottles—all this is seen against the underlying desire to kill for money.

Chaucer's account of the disintegration of the sworn brotherhood under the effects of avarice allows him to express sin in terms of character. The earlier sins of drunkenness and blasphemy have been left behind. This part of the tale is dealing with the more calculating side of human sin. The changes of emphasis and narrative speed in Chaucer can guide us in what is important. Here, it is the words of the three young men that condemn themselves, because Chaucer is interested in their motives. By contrast, the murder of the youngest, and the deaths of the other two from poison, are dismissed in a line or two. Indeed, the Pardoner makes it very conspicuous that he is not interested in the physical deaths:

What nedeth it to sermone of it moore?   (593)

Chaucer's Pardoner is interested in the *spiritual* deaths of his three revellers, and spiritual death can only be illustrated while they are still alive and able to destroy themselves by the sins they reveal in their speeches.

The sheer poetic justice of their end, and their own lack of names, means that the mechanism of the plot becomes the most memorable part of the tale. The whole story has the power to become an image in the mind, of the two who turned on the third and were themselves killed. The parallel with the blasphemous joke about the Trinity is intriguing. Chaucer makes his youngest man go to fetch bread and wine, the form in which Christ is represented in the Christian Mass, and this suggests that the Pardoner sees this larger pattern behind his tale of three riotous young men. As with the appearance of the Old Man in the story, Chaucer's tale here has the capacity to deal with extraordinary local vigour with details and patterns of plot and character which have universal resonance. The echo of the blasphemy reflects on the character of the Pardoner himself. For his own gain he uses a story which plays on the religious beliefs of his victims. But that story itself, at another level, represents the destruction of that Three-Personed Christian God, whose service the Pardoner so consistently corrupts.

The Pardoner's last gamble

In conclusion, it is necessary to assess the extraordinary conclusion of the tale. After the ends of the three young men, the Pardoner is still giving to the Canterbury pilgrims an example of his preaching. So he goes on to demonstrate how he exploits the emotions aroused by his tale, in order to persuade the ignorant people to give him their money in return for his pardon. First, he exclaims on the sins attacked by the story, moving his audience to repentance at the thought of how they betray Christ by their wickedness. The change of tone when the Pardoner attempts to convert this emotion into cash for himself is extremely crude:

Now, goode men, God foryeve yow youre trespas,
And ware yow fro the sinne of avarice!
Myn hooly pardoun may yow alle warice,
So that ye offre nobles or sterlinges.   (618–21)

But of course, the Pardoner has never pretended to his present audience that his methods are anything but crude. It is part of his boast, that by eloquence he is able to get away with such methods of exploitation. And so the Pardoner ends his 'sample' sermon, and turns back to address the pilgrims who have listened to him:

. . . And lo, sires, thus I preche.
And Jhesu Crist, that is oure soules leche,
So graunte yow his pardoun to receive,
For that is best; I wol yow nat deceive.   (629–32)

This passage has been seen as a moment of terrible sincerity by the Pardoner: he is revolted by the rehearsal of his own fraud that he has just finished and breaks down to urge the pilgrims to follow the true way of Christ.* The idea is attractive to modern readers for it gives the Pardoner a tragic regret. By this interpretation, he is able to see and repent of his own wickedness in misleading others. But unfortunately, this interpretation rests on the tone of voice with which one imagines the Pardoner speaking the lines, rather than upon any meaning which is very strongly present in the words themselves. Since we have already seen the Pardoner's skill in using religious language insincerely, it is an open question how sincere we can believe him to be here.

But now, in the most remarkable development, the Pardoner tries to sell his pardons to the Canterbury pilgrims, the same people who have just heard his contemptuous account of how he exploits the ignorant with those pardons. With this, Chaucer shows his Pardoner carried away by the energy of his own methods, just as he had earlier shown the Pardoner's happiness in his own skills. It is almost as if the Pardoner is drunk with the desire to make fools of others. It would be his supreme achievement to persuade the pilgrims to buy, when he has just shown them what fools anybody would be to buy from him. It would be the equivalent of selling a fool a medicine which will prevent him being

* G.L. Kittredge, *Chaucer and his Poetry*, Harvard University Press, Cambridge, Mass., 1927.

jealous, even though he knows he is right to be jealous! If this had succeeded, it would have been 'super-fraud'. It would mean that the Pardoner's powers to persuade were infinite, and with them his powers to control. Of course, he must fail. And Chaucer has already prepared the rock on which his ship will break: the common-sense figure of the Host. But it is quite appropriate to the self-destructive nature of the Pardoner's ambition to deceive, that he should himself choose the Host as his victim. In his pride, he has chosen the most difficult case. The sheer obscenity of the Host's verbal attack on the Pardoner is not simply there for its own sake. It is only the plainest language which can expose the deceptions on which the Pardoner lives. And the Host's rudeness goes straight to the two sides of the Pardoner: his homosexuality and his fraudulent relics. The complete scepticism of the Host simply destroys the confidence-tricks on which the Pardoner works. He reacts more strongly than the Host expects, but then the bases of his life and work have been threatened. He becomes angry, which is contrary to the atmosphere of game in which the Host is organising the competition of tales on the pilgrimage. Refusal to recognise game as game angers the Host in turn. It is this unexpected seriousness which the knight, as the person of highest rank on the pilgrimage, steps in to smooth over.

It is of course characteristic of the Pardoner that he is unable to see the joke in the Host's response. He bears resentment, just as the whole tale can be seen to result from his resentment when the *gentils* immediately think he will tell them a filthy story. He shows them a pardoner just as horrid as they expect. At first he tries to win social acceptability by showing them how detached he too is from the work he does. But at the end, the temptation to trick the upper classes as well as the lower, the temptation to trick the whole world, leads to his downfall. With the incongruous forced kiss between the Host and the Pardoner, this violent and disturbing Tale is brought to an end on a note of peace.

Part 4

Hints for study

Some suggestions for detailed study

The Pardoner's Character. The character of the Pardoner, in so many respects, *is* the Pardoner's tale. A detailed study of his character offers a good way to understand the tale that he tells. For it helps us to discern the framework in which are presented the sermon-material and the tale of the search for Death. It is necessary to take account of Chaucer's description of the Pardoner's appearance and manners, in the *General Prologue* to *The Canterbury Tales*. His physical appearance and his clothes would convey his homosexuality to a medieval audience. But as a pathetic contrast to this, there are his claims to relationships with women. Chaucer used the Pardoner's drunkenness to reinforce the way in which the character of his Pardoner illustrates the themes in the tale.

The relation between the Pardoner's character and his profession should also be studied in detail. His work is based on his false claims to be able to absolve people from their sins and his assumption of the preaching role of a priest. These are both instances of his fraud and deception.

But his work is based on the security that his audiences are too stupid to be aware of his fraud. A contempt for his audience and a confidence in his own superior ability is central to his character, and could be illustrated.

More particularly, his methods as a preacher repay close study—it is an art of deception. The reader should notice how the Pardoner is able to make a show and parade of his own learning, but he knows his audience cannot follow too much learning without interruptions. It is in these interruptions that the Pardoner's art as an effective preacher lies. Notice how frequently he changes his method, alternating between the abstract and the vividly detailed, between the general theme and the particular emotional appeal, between his preaching and its desired effect on the audience's purse.

Finally, the reader should study the Pardoner's motives in telling his tale. There is evidence that it is an attempted revenge on the more refined pilgrims for their distaste and distrust. It is possible the Pardoner attacks Pardoners to win their favour. There is the recurrent theme that the Pardoner knows (and is content to know) that he himself commits the sin against which he preaches so effectively.

Irony.   Irony is the expression of one's meaning by language of opposite or different tendency. The many levels of irony in the tale have at their centre this irony of the Pardoner's use for his own profit of the text 'The love of money is the root of all evils'. But the Pardoner also preaches against other sins which he commits himself. Most obvious of these is drunkenness. It could be that the proportions of the structure of the tale are explained because the Pardoner is drunk when telling the tale. Moreover, the Pardoner puts great emphasis on the sin of blasphemy—but his own life and profession are themselves a blasphemy. The tale has its existence because the Pardoner 'confesses' about his life. But it is a self-revelation without repentance, without regret. The Pardoner boasts that he can move others to repent without repenting himself. But this is itself ironic at his expense. It proves the limitation of his preaching that he cannot convert himself. Nor, in the end can he convert the pilgrims. Unlike the other Canterbury pilgrims he does not conclude his own tale, because the episode is brought to an end by the Knight. Again, this reflects ironically on the limitations of his rhetoric and his art.

Form and Meaning.   That the form and its meaning are *one* is the triumph of *The Pardoner's Tale*, and it is success worthy of close analysis. The main points lie in the way the *exemplum*, or story, of the search for Death is contained within a frame of preaching which expresses the character of the Pardoner and his profession. The variety in narrative speeds, the use of anti-climax and contrast of styles within the overall framework could be studied. The characterisation of the three revellers can be followed in the way it illustrates sin. To medieval man, sin had no identity in itself: it was defined by its negativity; it was an absence of good. Like the Pardoner himself, the three 'riotours' give themselves away by their speech. The Pardoner's speech is ordered into elaborate deceit: the revellers' language is violent and destructive. It is a catalogue of blasphemy.

And a blasphemous outlook on life soon allows other sins. The three revellers do not need 'characters' as in a novel, where we look for complexity and ambiguity. It is the point about the Pardoner's three villains that they only have character in so far as it characterises some of the typical evils of human nature.

Symbolism. The events and characters of his tale themselves reflect the outlook of the Pardoner's mind, and exist for his theme. Because of the framework of presentation in a sermon, and the horror of the tale of the search for Death, the characters, events, and scenes also have a quality which is mysterious. Vivid images flash in front of our eyes in a film-like way. They make their impact by their power to suggest much more than they directly say. The child with his idea of Death as a character and the Old Man could be studied more closely as symbols in the tale. Both could also be seen as aspects of a character of Death which never appears on-stage in the tale. But both youth and Old Man have the ability to reflect, which is not present in the three 'riotours'. They, by contrast, are characterised by their literal way of thinking, by their inability to perceive a larger spiritual reality in the events they encounter. It is Christian belief that attention to the letter and not to the spirit of things is fatal to the soul. All the contrasts between the Old Man and the three 'killers of Death' are significant here: they reflect ironically on the blindness of the three. Their inability to see beyond their belief that something with a name (like Death) must be a person like themselves is a curious combination of the amusing and the horrifying, and the sense of the ridiculous in *The Pardoner's Tale* could be looked at, for the way the Pardoner uses the repellent and revolting to enforce his point. For the Pardoner always has a lively sense of the real which, however, has the film-like power to point beyond itself: the bells outside the tavern; the young child's reference to his mother (possibly the Church); the gold at the end of the crooked path (of sin); the bread and wine; the wounded sides of the youngest of the three. Such details (and others) should be studied. They help the story to be vivid both as story and as symbol, and in *The Pardoner's Tale* story and symbol are closely interrelated with each other.

Some key quotations

The Pardoner's character

The Pardoner's appearance is described in the *General Prologue* to *The Canterbury Tales*:

> This Pardoner hadde heer as yelow as wex,
> But smothe it heeng as dooth a strike of flex;
> By ounces henge his lokkes that he hadde
> And therwith he his shuldres overspradde;
> But thinne it lay, by colpons oon and oon ...
>
> (*General Prologue*, 675–9)

A voys he hadde as smal as hath a goot.
No berd hadde he, ne nevere sholde have;
As smothe it was as it were late shave.
I trowe he were a gelding or a mare . . .   (*General Prologue*, 688–91)

The Pardoner's liking for drink, and his attempts at sexual boasting:

Nay, I wol drinke licour of the vine,
And have a joly wenche in every toun.   (166–7)

The Pardoner's attitude to his audiences of simple people and his preaching techniques:

I rekke nevere, whan that they been beried,
Though that hir soules goon a-blakeberied . . .   (119–20)
. . . For lewed peple loven tales olde;
Swiche thinges kan they wel reporte and holde.   (151–2)

The Pardoner's false claims to preaching and absolving:

I stonde lyk a clerk in my pulpet,
And whan the lewed peple is doun yset,
I preche so as ye han herd bifoore,
And telle an hundred false japes moore.   (105–8)

He absolves falsely in exchange for money:

And I assoille him by the auctoritee
Which that by bulle ygraunted was to me.   (101–2)
. . . I yow assoille by myn heigh power,
Yow that wol offre, as clene and eek as cleer
As ye were born . . .   (627–9)

The Pardoner reveals the irony of his work in preaching for gain:

I preche of no thing but for coveitise.
Therfore my theme is yet, and evere was,
Radix malorum est Cupiditas.
Thus kan I preche again that same vice
Which that I use, and that is avarice   (138–42)

Although a 'vicious' man, the Pardoner can make other people better by preaching:

But though myself be gilty in that sinne,
Yet kan I maken oother folk to twynne
From avarice, and soore to repente.
But that is nat my principal entente.   (143–6)

And so he claims he can tell the pilgrims a 'moral' tale despite himself:

> For though myself be a ful vicious man,
> A moral tale yet I yow telle kan.   (173–4)

At the end of his sermon he turns to the pilgrims with words which may represent his sincere feelings, or may show how easily he can use the appearance of sincerity by using solemn religious ideas:

> ... And lo, sires, thus I preche.
> And Jhesu Crist, that is oure soules leche,
> So graunte yow his pardoun to receive,
> For that is best; I wol yow nat deceive.   (629–32)

He tries to give his salesmanship the supreme test by selling pardons to the same people who have just heard his self-revelation:

> Looke which a seuretee is it to yow alle
> That I am in youre felaweshipe yfalle,
> That may assoille yow, bothe moore and lasse.   (651–3)

The Pardoner's preaching

Some examples of the Pardoner's preaching technique should include first his attack on blasphemy and his reason for it:

> Hir othes ben so grete and so dampnable,
> That it is grisly for to heere hem swere.
> Oure blissed Lordes body they totere–
> Hem thoughte that Jewes rente him noght ynough.   (186–9)

Other features of his preaching include his ability to show the revolting nature of the sins: for example, gluttony:

> Whan man so drinketh of the white and rede
> That of his throte he maketh his privee,
> Thurgh thilke cursed superfluitee.   (240–2);

or of cooking:

> Out of the harde bones knokke they
> The mary, for they caste noght awey
> That may go thurgh the golet softe and swoote.   (255–7)

The Pardoner can use humour to preach against the sin of drunkenness; but the humour has a real moral point in showing how man deprives himself of his distinctive human faculties by excessive drink:

> Sour is thy breeth, foul artow to embrace,
> And thurgh thy dronke nose semeth the soun
> As though thou seydest ay 'Sampsoun, Sampsoun!'   (266–8)

Above all, the Pardoner is a master of the art of using exclamation and manipulating his audience's feelings. An example would be the climax of his sermon where he begins very generally ('O cursed sinne of alle cursednesse!') but concludes with a reproach to the audience for their unkindness to Christ ('Allas! mankinde, how may it bitide / That to thy creatour . . . Thou art so fals and so unkinde, allas?'—609ff.).

The Pardoner's Tale

In the tale itself, compare the revellers' blasphemous speeches with the way the child and Old Man speak. The child warns:

> Me thinketh that it were necessarie
> For to be war of swich an adversarie.
> Beth redy for to meete him everemoore;
> Thus taughte me my dame; I sey namoore.   (395–8)

It is the child's description of Death which impresses the 'riotours':

> Ther cam a privee theef men clepeth Deeth,
> That in the contree al the peple sleeth,
> And with his spere he smoot his herte atwo,
> And wente his wey withouten wordes mo.   (389–92)

The Old Man's description of himself with his stick is comparably vivid yet symbolic:

> And on the ground, which is my moodres gate,
> I knokke with my staf, bothe erly and late,
> And seye, 'Leeve mooder, leet me in!'   (443–5)

And he politely answers the request for directions to Death: for Death is always waiting at the end of the path of sin. The landscape is vivid, but the meaning is timeless:

> 'Now, sires,' quod he, 'if that yow be so leef
> To finde Deeth, turne up this croked wey,
> For in that grove I lafte him, by my fey,
> Under a tree, and there he wole abide'.   (474–7)

Note the interest in speed and movement in the tale:

> And everich of thise riotoures ran
> Til he cam to that tree ... (482–3)

But the Pardoner is also a master of the change of speed, as when he expresses the fact very quickly that the three give up looking for death—because they have found it:

> No lenger thanne after Deeth they soughte (486)

As the gold has its evil effect, notice how the revellers are exposed by their own speech: the youngest expresses his ambitions to himself in religious language because this shows ironically his completely material outlook, and consequently his damnation. It is a perversion of prayer:

> 'O Lord!' quod he, 'if so were that I mighte
> Have al this tresor to myself allone,
> Ther is no man that liveth under the trone
> Of God that sholde live so murye as I'. (554–7)

The murderous plan of the other two involves a deception of the youngest of the three, and in his death an echo of Christ's crucifixion.

> Aris as though thou woldest with him pleye,
> And I shal rive him thurgh the sides tweye. (541–2)

Finally, notice how the Pardoner dismisses the three to the deaths they have given each other:

> What nedeth it to sermone of it moore?
> For right as they hadde caste his deeth bifoore,
> Right so they han him slain, and that anon ... (593–5)

Destroyed in their own evil, the three deserve no further attention, the Pardoner's style implies:

> Thus ended been thise homicides two,
> And eek the false empoisonere also. (607–8)

Some questions and answers

The suggestions for detailed study will have indicated already some of the main areas of critical interest in *The Pardoner's Tale*. Some account would need to be taken of these in most answers on the poem. Some useful general guidelines are suggested by the nature of the work. It is a poem in which the teller of the tale is dramatised and characterised by the telling of that tale. And he tells the tale to show off his art. Chaucer's use of the character of the Pardoner, and the importance of the Pardoner's self-conscious use of his art, are the two outer frameworks to all our other responses to the tale. This is inevitable, since it is through the Pardoner and his nature that the tale presents itself.

'Discuss the role of the Pardoner in his tale'

In answering such a question, we want to be as thorough as Chaucer, who has built up a character and a type of a profession both before the tale starts and during it. We start with the *General Prologue* portrait: the suggestions of physical and spiritual eunuchry; the pride in deception and fraud. The tale is then seen as an extension of this character. But it is the Prologue to the tale, with its boasting and pride in fraud as a profitable trade, which gives an added ironic dimension to the tale, which is in itself a very moral *exemplum*. The preaching and the tale of the three revellers are now seen as aspects of the Pardoner's character. His learning and his understanding of sin and temptation continue his theme of being able to convert others, but not himself. Although the Pardoner is so self-aware in his sinfulness, his sin inevitably means that he is not so self-aware as he would be without sin. For true self-awareness would bring penitence, in the knowledge of one's own human wretchedness. The famous conclusion with the Pardoner's attempt to sell even to those who would know their own stupidity in buying from him, can be seen as the Pardoner's class-revenge on those who have despised him. It can also be seen as the failure of pure rhetoric. Chaucer is suggesting the limitations of rhetoric to persuade against all odds, although he has certainly illustrated how far the art may be carried beyond any relation to the truth or to the speaker's sincerity.

'Discuss the role of preaching in the tale'

Here the student could start with the Pardoner's own professional concern with preaching, and the illegality of his preaching. His response to the request for a moral tale is to give an example of his own sermons. It is something he knows by heart. This explains its extraordinary fluency. Now discuss how the sermon pattern affects the structure of the tale. Narrative example, both short and long, is contained within the overall framework of a sermon. Show how the sins illustrated by the Pardoner are closely tied to the *exemplum* of the three revellers. This prepares us to see their story in a moralistic light. Give some illustration of the skill and variation by which the Pardoner holds attention, of how he moves his audience against sin by example, by show of learning, by horror and by humour. Show how the attempt to kill Death is constructed and organised to emphasise the ironies at the expense of the revellers. The characters are being used not for themselves, but for the purpose of the preacher and his interest in temptation. Illustrate how the characters and their lives become symbolic in the tale. Finally, discuss the Pardoner's own attempt to extend his preaching from an ignorant to a sophisticated audience.

'How effective is the characterisation in *The Pardoner's Tale*?'

The effectiveness depends on what part in the Tale it is playing. (Characterisation in medieval works may play a very different role from that in later literature.) Given the framework of the Tale and its roots in preaching, the characterisation within the Tale represents ideas and forces in the mind of the Pardoner. The impact of the characters depends on their thematic importance. This explains the differences between them. The innocence of the child can be represented by a mysterious, wondering speech which is fairly brief (illustrate). The child has no other role but this one, significant appearance. Similarly with the Old Man, with whom the child forms a contrast. He has only one, dramatic and memorable appearance, although the range of meanings suggested is much larger, and the speech much longer, reflecting the appearance of age (illustrate). Compare the influential role of the Old Man in suggesting reflection, with the accounts of the sources. The child and the Old Man dramatise choices and turning-points for the 'riotours'. Compare the sources again on the interest in their choices and their temptations: for example, in the brotherhood to kill death; and in the planned murders of their 'brothers'. Illustrate their characters through the sins that appear in their speech. But also illustrate how their characters only interest the Pardoner as long as they concern his theme: his interest in their plans to murder contrasted with his lack of interest in their deaths. Show how the Pardoner's characterisation works by strong contrasts. Conclude on the way the characterisation partly embodies the sins of the character of the Pardoner.

Part 5

Suggestions for further reading

The text

SPEARING, A.C. (ED.): *The Pardoner's Prologue and Tale*, Cambridge University Press, Cambridge, 1965.

Background to Chaucer

BREWER, D.S.: *Chaucer in his Time*, Longman, London, 1973.

BREWER, D.S. (ED.): *Writers and Their Background: Geoffrey Chaucer*, Bell, London, 1974.

MILLER, R.P.: *Chaucer Sources and Backgrounds*, Oxford University Press, New York, 1977.

RICKERT, E.: *Chaucer's World*, Columbia University Press, New York, 1948.

ROBERTSON, D.W.: *A Preface to Chaucer*, Princeton University Press, Princeton, New Jersey, 1962.

SPEARING, A.C.: *Criticism and Medieval Poetry*, Edward Arnold, London, 1972.

Some Modern Critical Work on Chaucer

BREWER, D.S.: *Chaucer*, Longman; 3rd edn., London, 1973.

BOWDEN, M.: *A Commentary on The General Prologue to The Canterbury Tales*, Souvenir Press, London, 1973.

BROOKS, H.F.: *Chaucer's Pilgrims*, Methuen, London, 1962.

DONALDSON, E.T.: *Speaking of Chaucer*, Athlone Press, London, 1970.

EVANS, G.: *Chaucer*, Blackie & Son, London, 1977.

HOWARD, D.R.: *The Idea of The Canterbury Tales*, University of California Press, Berkeley, California, 1976.

HUSSEY, S.S.: *An Introduction to Chaucer*, Methuen, London, 1971.

KEAN, P.M.: *Chaucer and the Making of English Poetry*, Routledge and Kegan Paul, London, 1972.

LAWLOR, J.: *Chaucer*, Hutchinson, London, 1968.

PAYNE, R.O.: *The Key of Remembrance*, Yale University Press, New Haven and London, 1963.

RUGGIERS, P.G.: *The Art of The Canterbury Tales*, University of Wisconsin Press, Madison, 1965.

WHITTOCK, T.: *A Reading of The Canterbury Tales*, Cambridge University Press, Cambridge, 1970.

The author of these notes

Dr B.A. Windeatt was educated at the University of Cambridge, where he read English for his first degree. He stayed at Cambridge to undertake research in the field of medieval literature, and now lives and teaches English there. His particular interests have been in the relationships between medieval English literature and the literature of medieval France and Italy, and he is at present engaged on the preparation of a new edition of Chaucer's poem *Troilus and Criseyde*.

York Notes: list of titles

CHINUA ACHEBE
A Man of the People
Arrow of God
Things Fall Apart

EDWARD ALBEE
Who's Afraid of Virginia Woolf?

ELECHI AMADI
The Concubine

ANONYMOUS
Beowulf
Everyman

JOHN ARDEN
Serjeant Musgrave's Dance

AYI KWEI ARMAH
The Beautyful Ones Are Not Yet Born

W. H. AUDEN
Selected Poems

JANE AUSTEN
Emma
Mansfield Park
Northanger Abbey
Persuasion
Pride and Prejudice
Sense and Sensibility

HONORÉ DE BALZAC
Le Père Goriot

SAMUEL BECKETT
Waiting for Godot

SAUL BELLOW
Henderson, The Rain King

ARNOLD BENNETT
Anna of the Five Towns

WILLIAM BLAKE
Songs of Innocence, Songs of Experience

ROBERT BOLT
A Man For All Seasons

ANNE BRONTË
The Tenant of Wildfell Hall

CHARLOTTE BRONTË
Jane Eyre

EMILY BRONTË
Wuthering Heights

ROBERT BROWNING
Men and Women

JOHN BUCHAN
The Thirty-Nine Steps

JOHN BUNYAN
The Pilgrim's Progress

BYRON
Selected Poems

ALBERT CAMUS
L'Etranger (The Outsider)

GEOFFREY CHAUCER
Prologue to the Canterbury Tales
The Franklin's Tale
The Knight's Tale
The Merchant's Tale
The Miller's Tale
The Nun's Priest's Tale
The Pardoner's Tale
The Wife of Bath's Tale
Troilus and Criseyde

ANTON CHEKHOV
The Cherry Orchard

SAMUEL TAYLOR COLERIDGE
Selected Poems

WILKIE COLLINS
The Moonstone
The Woman in White

SIR ARTHUR CONAN DOYLE
The Hound of the Baskervilles

WILLIAM CONGREVE
The Way of the World

JOSEPH CONRAD
Heart of Darkness
Lord Jim
Nostromo
The Secret Agent
Victory
Youth and *Typhoon*

STEPHEN CRANE
The Red Badge of Courage

BRUCE DAWE
Selected Poems

WALTER DE LA MARE
Selected Poems

DANIEL DEFOE
A Journal of the Plague Year
Moll Flanders
Robinson Crusoe

CHARLES DICKENS
A Tale of Two Cities
Bleak House
David Copperfield
Great Expectations
Hard Times
Little Dorrit
Nicholas Nickleby
Oliver Twist
Our Mutual Friend
The Pickwick Papers

EMILY DICKINSON
Selected Poems

JOHN DONNE
Selected Poems

THEODORE DREISER
Sister Carrie

GEORGE ELIOT
Adam Bede
Middlemarch
Silas Marner
The Mill on the Floss

T. S. ELIOT
Four Quartets
Murder in the Cathedral
Selected Poems
The Cocktail Party
The Waste Land

J. G. FARRELL
The Siege of Krishnapur

GEORGE FARQUHAR
The Beaux Stratagem

WILLIAM FAULKNER
Absalom, Absalom!
As I Lay Dying
Go Down, Moses
The Sound and the Fury

HENRY FIELDING
Joseph Andrews
Tom Jones

F. SCOTT FITZGERALD
Tender is the Night
The Great Gatsby

E. M. FORSTER
A Passage to India
Howards End

ATHOL FUGARD
Selected Plays

JOHN GALSWORTHY
Strife

MRS GASKELL
North and South

WILLIAM GOLDING
Lord of the Flies
The Inheritors
The Spire

OLIVER GOLDSMITH
She Stoops to Conquer
The Vicar of Wakefield

ROBERT GRAVES
Goodbye to All That

GRAHAM GREENE
Brighton Rock
The Heart of the Matter
The Power and the Glory

THOMAS HARDY
Far from the Madding Crowd
Jude the Obscure
Selected Poems
Tess of the D'Urbervilles
The Mayor of Casterbridge
The Return of the Native
The Trumpet Major
The Woodlanders
Under the Greenwood Tree

L. P. HARTLEY
The Go-Between
The Shrimp and the Anemone

NATHANIEL HAWTHORNE
The Scarlet Letter

SEAMUS HEANEY
Selected Poems

ERNEST HEMINGWAY
A Farewell to Arms
For Whom the Bell Tolls
The African Stories
The Old Man and the Sea

GEORGE HERBERT
Selected Poems

HERMANN HESSE
Steppenwolf

BARRY HINES
Kes

HOMER
The Iliad

ANTHONY HOPE
The Prisoner of Zenda

GERARD MANLEY HOPKINS
Selected Poems

WILLIAM DEAN HOWELLS
The Rise of Silas Lapham

RICHARD HUGHES
A High Wind in Jamaica

THOMAS HUGHES
Tom Brown's Schooldays

ALDOUS HUXLEY
Brave New World

HENRIK IBSEN
A Doll's House
Ghosts
Hedda Gabler

HENRY JAMES
Daisy Miller
The Europeans
The Portrait of a Lady
The Turn of the Screw
Washington Square

SAMUEL JOHNSON
Rasselas

BEN JONSON
The Alchemist
Volpone

JAMES JOYCE
A Portrait of the Artist as a Young Man
Dubliners

JOHN KEATS
Selected Poems

RUDYARD KIPLING
Kim

D. H. LAWRENCE
Sons and Lovers
The Rainbow
Women in Love

CAMARA LAYE
L'Enfant Noir

HARPER LEE
To Kill a Mocking-Bird

LAURIE LEE
Cider with Rosie

THOMAS MANN
Tonio Kröger

CHRISTOPHER MARLOWE
Doctor Faustus
Edward II

ANDREW MARVELL
Selected Poems

W. SOMERSET MAUGHAM
Of Human Bondage
Selected Short Stories

J. MEADE FALKNER
Moonfleet

HERMAN MELVILLE
Billy Budd
Moby Dick

THOMAS MIDDLETON
Women Beware Women

THOMAS MIDDLETON *and* WILLIAM ROWLEY
The Changeling

ARTHUR MILLER
Death of a Salesman
The Crucible

JOHN MILTON
Paradise Lost I & II
Paradise Lost IV & IX
Selected Poems

V. S. NAIPAUL
A House for Mr Biswas

SEAN O'CASEY
Juno and the Paycock
The Shadow of a Gunman

GABRIEL OKARA
The Voice

EUGENE O'NEILL
Mourning Becomes Electra

GEORGE ORWELL
Animal Farm
Nineteen Eighty-four

JOHN OSBORNE
Look Back in Anger

WILFRED OWEN
Selected Poems

ALAN PATON
Cry, The Beloved Country

THOMAS LOVE PEACOCK
Nightmare Abbey and *Crotchet Castle*

HAROLD PINTER
The Birthday Party
The Caretaker

PLATO
The Republic

ALEXANDER POPE
Selected Poems

THOMAS PYNCHON
The Crying of Lot 49

SIR WALTER SCOTT
Ivanhoe
Quentin Durward
The Heart of Midlothian
Waverley

PETER SHAFFER
The Royal Hunt of the Sun

WILLIAM SHAKESPEARE
A Midsummer Night's Dream
Antony and Cleopatra
As You Like It
Coriolanus
Cymbeline
Hamlet
Henry IV Part I
Henry IV Part II
Henry V
Julius Caesar
King Lear
Love's Labour's Lost
Macbeth
Measure for Measure
Much Ado About Nothing
Othello
Richard II
Richard III
Romeo and Juliet
Sonnets
The Merchant of Venice
The Taming of the Shrew
The Tempest
The Winter's Tale
Troilus and Cressida
Twelfth Night
The Two Gentlemen of Verona

GEORGE BERNARD SHAW
Androcles and the Lion
Arms and the Man
Caesar and Cleopatra
Candida
Major Barbara
Pygmalion
Saint Joan
The Devil's Disciple

MARY SHELLEY
Frankenstein

PERCY BYSSHE SHELLEY
Selected Poems

RICHARD BRINSLEY SHERIDAN
The School for Scandal
The Rivals

WOLE SOYINKA
The Lion and the Jewel
The Road
Three Short Plays

EDMUND SPENSER
The Faerie Queene (Book I)

JOHN STEINBECK
Of Mice and Men
The Grapes of Wrath
The Pearl

LAURENCE STERNE
A Sentimental Journey
Tristram Shandy

ROBERT LOUIS STEVENSON
Kidnapped
Treasure Island
Dr Jekyll and Mr Hyde

TOM STOPPARD
Professional Foul
Rosencrantz and Guildenstern are Dead

JONATHAN SWIFT
Gulliver's Travels

JOHN MILLINGTON SYNGE
The Playboy of the Western World

TENNYSON
Selected Poems

W. M. THACKERAY
Vanity Fair

DYLAN THOMAS
Under Milk Wood

EDWARD THOMAS
Selected Poems

FLORA THOMPSON
Lark Rise to Candleford

J. R. R. TOLKIEN
The Hobbit
The Lord of the Rings

CYRIL TOURNEUR
The Revenger's Tragedy

ANTHONY TROLLOPE
Barchester Towers

MARK TWAIN
Huckleberry Finn
Tom Sawyer

VIRGIL
The Aeneid

VOLTAIRE
Candide

EVELYN WAUGH
Decline and Fall
A Handful of Dust

JOHN WEBSTER
The Duchess of Malfi
The White Devil

H. G. WELLS
The History of Mr Polly
The Invisible Man
The War of the Worlds

ARNOLD WESKER
Chips with Everything
Roots

PATRICK WHITE
Voss

OSCAR WILDE
The Importance of Being Earnest

TENNESSEE WILLIAMS
The Glass Menagerie

VIRGINIA WOOLF
To the Lighthouse

WILLIAM WORDSWORTH
Selected Poems

W. B. YEATS
Selected Poems